THREE DISCOURSES

THOMAS HOBBES

THREE
DISCOURSES

A Critical Modern Edition
of Newly Identified Work
of the Young Hobbes

Edited by
Noel B. Reynolds and Arlene W. Saxonhouse

THE UNIVERSITY OF CHICAGO PRESS
Chicago and London

NOEL B. REYNOLDS, professor of political science at Brigham Young University, specializes in wordprinting analysis.
ARLENE W. SAXONHOUSE is James O. Murfin professor of political science at the University of Michigan.

The University of Chicago Press, Chicago 60637
The University of Chicago Press, Ltd., London
©1995 by the University of Chicago
All rights reserved. Published 1995
Printed in the United States of America
04 03 02 01 00 99 98 97 96 95   1 2 3 4 5

ISBN: 0-226-34545-9 (cloth)

Facsimiles from the first printed edition of the *Discourses* courtesy Special Collections, The University of Chicago Libraries.

Library of Congress Cataloging-in-Publication Data

Hobbes, Thomas, 1588–1679.
    Thomas Hobbes : three discourses : a critical modern edition of
newly identified work of the young Hobbes / edited by Noel B.
Reynolds and Arlene W. Saxonhouse.
        p.   cm.
    Includes bibliographical references (p.   ) and index.
    ISBN 0-226-34545-9 (acid-free paper)
    1. Political science—Early works to 1800.   2. Hobbes, Thomas,
1588–1679—Contributions in political science.   3. Hobbes, Thomas,
1588–1679—Authorship.   I. Reynolds, Noel B.   II. Saxonhouse,
Arlene W.   III. Title.
JC153.H515   1995
320.1'092—dc20   95-12724

CONTENTS

Preface   vii

PART ONE

Hobbes and the *Horae Subsecivae*   3

PART TWO

Three Discourses by Thomas Hobbes   23
A Note on Editing Principles   23
Introduction to the *Horae Subsecivae* by Edward Blount   27
A Discourse upon the Beginning of Tacitus   31
A Discourse of Rome   71
A Discourse of Laws   105

PART THREE

**Hobbes and the Beginnings of
Modern Political Thought   123**

PART FOUR

Statistical Wordprinting   157

Appendixes
1. Table of Contents of the 1620 *Horae Subsecivae*   163
2. Texts and Word Blocks Analyzed   164
3. List of 65 Noncontextual-Word Patterns   166

Bibliography   171

Index   177

PREFACE

THIS EDITION of Hobbes's *Discourses* owes its origins to a 1988 conference in Colorado Springs organized by Timothy Fuller on the political thought of Michael Oakeshott. It was there that Noel Reynolds and Arlene Saxonhouse met and, over one of the lunches, discussed Hobbes and Saxonhouse's almost forgotten dissertation on the *Horae Subsecivae: Observations and Discourses.* Saxonhouse told Reynolds of her efforts to argue that the small 1620 volume was the work of Thomas Hobbes, and of her difficulty in convincing others on the basis of historical, archival, and textual evidence that this was the case. Prospective publishers complained that there was no "smoking gun," that they could not risk publishing such a work by a recent Ph.D. who was not yet, as one editor put it, "a scholar of overriding distinction." Finding herself in a catch-22, Saxonhouse let the thesis lie largely ignored, and efforts to publish the *Horae Subsecivae* in a modern edition were abandoned.

Fortuitously, Reynolds was closely involved with statisticians at Brigham Young University who have done some of the most important work in developing statistical techniques for identifying authorship for disputed texts, or "wordprinting." Reynolds persuaded John L. Hilton to join him in what became a four-year project, the many findings of which have been reported in conferences and journal publications over the last two years.

The results relative to the *Horae Subsecivae* were both exhil-

vii

arating and disappointing. The three discourses published here could confidently be attributed to Hobbes, but the volume's twelve shorter essays or observations which draw heavily on Baconian themes and language, portraying the passionate young aristocrat with all his foibles, and the fourth discourse, were authored by someone else—perhaps Hobbes's tutee, but clearly not Hobbes himself.

While it would have been more satisfying to have the entire work match Hobbes's later writings, we thought that the identification of the three discourses as previously unrecognized and unacknowledged Hobbesian works was of great significance and that they were worthy of republication. These three discourses give us direct access to Hobbes's intellectual concerns and motivating interests at a point almost two decades earlier than was possible through his previously recognized writings.

Many individuals and institutions have helped produce this volume. Most significantly, we thank John Hilton, without whose generous efforts and statistical expertise the study could never have been accomplished. Reynolds thanks his daughter Rebecca, whose historical and linguistic skills were essential in editing the Hobbes text and producing the explanatory footnotes, and undergraduate research assistants Mark Freeman, Julianne Nuzman, Kylie Nielson Turley, and Cody Winchester, who each contributed substantially to this project. He also expresses appreciation to Noel Malcolm, who generously shared his vast knowledge of Hobbes history and texts in helping us to avoid mistakes and to strengthen arguments. John F. Hall served willingly as a final court of appeal on difficult matters of Roman history or Latin translation. Brigham Young University colleagues Madison U. Sowell, De Lamar Jensen, and Carma DeJong Anderson provided free consulting services on questions involving Italian language, Italian history, and antique costumes respectively. Marilyn Webb gave extensive assistance with the scanning of texts, and Joyce V. Penrod and Deans Donovan Fleming and Clayne L. Pope demonstrated continuing support in arranging for research support from Brigham Young University.

Saxonhouse enjoyed the research and editorial support of Ted Clayton, Eric Kos, Shannetta Paskel, and Gary Shiffman.

She received generous funding from the Office of the Vice-President for Research at the University of Michigan in support of the project. Saxonhouse appreciates the early encouragement to work on the *Horae Subsecivae* she received as a graduate student at Yale University from Professors Joseph Hamburger and Marvin Kendrick. She also thanks Thomas Foster for a friendship that has included, among much else, protection from egregious and not so egregious errors of grammar and style.

We also wish to thank Tim Fuller for arranging the Liberty Fund conference that serendipitously led to this project. Reynolds registers special thanks to his wife, Sydney, for her unstinting support in this among countless other research projects, and particularly in this one for her proofreading of the Hobbes text one seventeenth-century word at a time. Saxonhouse would also like to thank her husband, Gary, who has lived with (and speculated on) the question of Hobbesian authorship of the *Horae Subsecivae* for more years than he may care to remember and who, as she noted in her acknowledgments to her original thesis, "took his innumerable turns to read the *Tale of Benjamin Bunny* innumerable times" so that the work could be completed. Beatrix Potter is no longer part of his repertoire, but the loving support still is.

PART ONE

HOBBES
AND THE
Horae Subsecivae

HOBBES
AND THE
Horae Subsecivae

Noel B. Reynolds and Arlene W. Saxonhouse

I N 1620 IN LONDON, a small volume of essays and discourses appeared anonymously. The publisher, a Mr. Edward Blount, introduced the compact volume by noting that, though he knew not the author, he had heard by chance that a friend had "some such papers" and he had heard them commended; he read them and concluded that "they would be welcome abroad." His "friend's courtesy bestowed" a copy freely on him, and in his endeavor to give his readers "contentment," he published the collection of, as he calls it, "mixed matter." Recent wordprint studies on the question of the authorship of this volume now show that Mr. Blount's decision to give his readers "contentment" has also provided those of us living more than three and a half centuries later with unprecedented access to the early writings and thought of Thomas Hobbes. The three discourses published here for the first time under Hobbes's name were originally part of Blount's small volume entitled *Horae Subsecivae: Observations and Discourses*.[1] The en-

---

1 The Latin words in this title mean "leisure hours"; the phrase "tempora subsecivae" appears at the beginning of Cicero's *de Legibus* (I.iii.9), and the

3

tire work consists of twelve essays or "observations" reminiscent in style and language of Bacon's essays and devoted to such topics as arrogance, expenses, reading history, religion, and death, and four much longer discourses, three of which we have been able to attribute to Hobbes.[2]

Leo Strauss (1952 [1936], xii, n. 1) first suggested that the *Horae Subsecivae* might be of Hobbesian authorship. During his research at the library at Chatsworth, the country estate in Derbyshire where Hobbes spent most of his life as a tutor and family retainer to the Cavendish family, Strauss came upon an abbreviated manuscript version of ten of the twelve observations included in the *Horae Subsecivae*. The manuscript, entitled simply "Essayes," is, according to Strauss and others, written in Hobbes's hand and is signed as "this dayes present" to William Cavendish, first earl of Devonshire, by his son, who was also named William Cavendish. The son, later to be the second earl of Devonshire, was Hobbes's tutee. The essays in the manu-

---

editor of the Loeb edition notes that "subsecivae" was originally a technical term used by surveyors to refer to small pieces of land which were left over in their surveys. The *Oxford English Dictionary (OED)* indicates that "subsecivae" was commonly used in the early seventeenth century to refer to things left over, and especially to vacant hours. The complete Table of Contents of the *Horae Subsecivae* can be found in Appendix 1 below.

2 Supporting Strauss's claim that the "Essayes" are in Hobbes's handwriting are Wolf (1969, 116), who reprints the manuscript in its entirety, and Peter Beal, the compiler of *English Literary Manuscripts*, who writes in a personal letter (26 September 1992) to Reynolds: "I spent a considerable period of time studying all known Hobbes MSS, and all the MSS at Chatsworth, and came to know and to recognise his hand very well indeed. I puzzled long over the *Horae*, but eventually came to the definite conclusion that it was a fair copy in Hobbes's hand—of that I have no doubt, and you can quote me on that." In his earlier published note on these "Essayes" Beal observed that they were "written throughout in the early formal hand of Hobbes" (1987, 2:583). See also Harwood (1986, 26–27), who supports the claims that the "Essayes" are in Hobbes's hand, Parry (1971, 250) who accepts the claim, and Bush (1973, 163) who has no particular opinion of the claim but questions whether the conclusion that the manuscript is in Hobbes's hand makes any difference regarding Hobbesian authorship. Strauss's and Wolf's claim concerning the handwriting is contested by Rogow (1986, 249–50), who nevertheless suggests that the marginal notes written in the volume of the *Horae Subsecivae* kept at Chatsworth may have been in Hobbes's hand, and Hamilton (1978, 451–52), who thinks the "Essayes" is simply a handwritten copy of the printed version. As Bush notes, handwriting does not prove authorship. Noel Malcolm in his

script appear to have been written after the 1612 publication of Bacon's *Essays* and after the Continental trip taken by William Cavendish, the future second earl, and Hobbes, dating the essays to the middle of the second decade of the seventeenth century.[3] These dates for the composition of the work confirm that the "Essayes" were dedicated by the William Cavendish who was Hobbes's tutee, rather than by his father, the first earl.[4]

The discovery of these essays at Chatsworth and later the discovery that they appeared in print in the published version of the *Horae Subsecivae* aroused Strauss's speculation as to whether the *Horae Subsecivae* might indeed be the work of Hobbes and thus give us insight into his early thought. This would have been of much interest to a scholar such as Strauss who focused on discovering Hobbes's moral attitude prior to his infatuation with the natural sciences and geometric method. Oakeshott, in his introduction to his edition of *Leviathan*, laments that when Hobbes appears as a philosophical writer, "He is already adult, mature in mind; the eager period of search, of tentative experiment, goes unreflected in his pages" (1946, xiv). One of the peculiarities in studying Hobbes is that apart from a poem entitled *de Mirabilibus Pecci,* which extols the scenic beauty of the Derbyshire countryside, nothing remains to help us understand his early intellectual development and the influences upon his thought before the translation of Thucydides in 1627, when Hobbes was almost forty years old.[5]

Early works written by Hobbes prior to 1620 would present us with special access to his speculations on questions of politi-

---

forthcoming biography of Hobbes presents convincing evidence that the essays were copied in a fair hand by Hobbes from a rough draft written by someone else, most likely by William Cavendish, who would have been the only person who had access to Hobbes's services for such a task (personal communication to Reynolds from Malcolm, 28 June 1993).

3   Malcolm (1981, 320–21).

4   Wolf (1969, 133–34) reprints the speculation of Francis Thompson, former librarian at Chatsworth, concerning which William Cavendish signed the "dayes present" to his father. See also Malcolm (1981, 320–21).

5   Malcolm (1981) explores the interesting possibility that Hobbes's attendance at the meetings of the Virginia Company might give some insight into his early thought on the issues of natural right and natural law that were at the core of the company's claims to possess the land it was colonizing.

cal philosophy prior to his famed "discovery of geometry" in a
gentleman's library somewhere on the Continent at the age of
forty.[6] We would then be in a position to evaluate early influences on his thought and assess the ways in which the political
experiences of his time and his exposure to a new methodological approach influenced (or did not influence) his political
philosophy. So much of the scholarship on Hobbes has focused on his methodological innovations, on his application
of science and the deductive method to the study of politics,
that at times the significance of his political philosophy has
been lost in this fascination with his method.[7] When the discipline of political science was itself entranced with its own move
to a methodology that derived from science in its universal abstraction from particulars, Hobbes became something of a
hero who, while not necessarily successful in applying such a
method to the study of politics, nevertheless recognized its possibilities (Goldsmith 1966; McNeilly 1968; Peters 1956; Watkins 1965). More recently, some scholars have mined the
rational-choice potential in Hobbes (Gauthier 1969; Hampton
1986; Kavka 1986; Talaska 1988), while others continue to
probe the scientific sources of Hobbes's thought (Sorrell
1986; Tuck 1988).[8]

6 This is charmingly described by Aubrey (1898, 1:332): "Being in a gentleman's library in . . . , Euclid's Elements lay open, and 'twas the 47 El. libri I.
He read the proposition. 'By G—. . . .' sayd he, 'this is impossible!' So he reads
the demonstration of it, which referred him back to such a proposition. . . . Et
sic Deinceps, that at last he was demonstratively convinced of that trueth. This
made him in love with geometry." In his prose autobiography, Hobbes himself
describes his delight at his discovery of Euclid (*delectatus methodo illius*), in particular, on account of the "*artem ratiocinandi*" (Hobbes 1839, 1:xiv; future references to this work will be to *LW,* for *Latin Works*).
7 For early expressions see, for example, Laird (1934, v), Stephen ([1904]
1961, 17), or Taylor (1908, 28). It was such readings as these that led to
Strauss's desire to show the moral foundations of Hobbes's thought.
8 Hobbes himself is in large part responsible for those interpretations that
dismiss his early thought and emphasize the importance of method in his
thought. He cites his encounter with the French friar Marin Mersenne and his
circle of Parisian intellectuals as the point from which he was numbered
among philosophers (*tempore ab illo/ Inter philosophos et numebar ego* [*LW* 1:xc]).
Strauss rejects this disjunction; see also Johnston (1986) for a more recent
reading of Hobbes that denies the sharp break between the early and the "scientific" Hobbes.

Part III of this volume argues that Hobbes's significance comes not only from his unique methodology, from his attempt to bring deductive, axiomatic reasoning to the study of politics and thereby create "political science," but from his exposition of the central principles of modern political thought—in particular, the concern with the principles of political foundation in a world independent of any divine order. This outlook, one in radical opposition to medieval and classical thought, first appears in Machiavelli's work about a century earlier. It reappears forcefully at the core of Hobbes's thought before Euclid and before Mersenne enter his life.[9] The computerized wordprint analysis of the *Horae Subsecivae* enables us to support such a claim about the development and significance of Hobbes's thought. By identifying the three discourses published there as statistically indistinguishable from Hobbes's other writings, we have gained access to Hobbes's early writings on which such an assertion must be based.

The *Horae Subsecivae* as a whole has been attributed to a number of possible authors over the centuries, but only with Strauss's discovery of the "Essayes" has the debate centered around Hobbesian authorship. Efforts to identify the author of the often charming essays and provocative reflections in the *Horae Subsecivae* began almost immediately after its anonymous publication by Mr. Blount. During the seventeenth century, the work was clearly associated with the Cavendish family of Chatsworth in Derbyshire. The earliest published reference of

---

In his writings Hobbes frequently emphasizes that it is his method above all which distinguishes him from all other moral philosophers and makes his thought certain in a way that no other moral philosopher's could be, and he apologizes that he had to delay the publication of *De Corpore*, his study of method, by some fifteen to twenty years because of the civil war in England (*LW* 1:xc–xcii). See also, *De Corpore* I.i.1 (Hobbes 1966, 1:2 [future references to this work will be to *EW*, for *English Works*]; *De Cive*, To the Reader [*EW* 2:xi]; *Leviathan*, 31). See further below, Part III, p. 140–41.

9 Because of the focus on Hobbes's innovative methodological approach to politics, the relationship between his thought and that of Machiavelli has been almost entirely disregarded or, if not disregarded, then dismissed (Meinecke 1957, 210–16; Raab 1964, 192–200; Watkins 1965, 37). The historical method of Machiavelli and Hobbes's deductivism and debunking of history (see, however, Johnston 1986, chap. 1) make the differences between their approaches to politics appear far greater than they are. Part III below explores

which we are aware assigns one of the four discourses to William Cavendish, Hobbes's charge (Willard 1914, 109)[10] and at least among the Cavendishes the book was attributed to William. A copy of the *Horae Subsecivae* kept at Chatsworth has the inscription on the title page "written by Cavendysh."[11] In a catalogue from about 1660 of books kept in the library of the Cavendishes at Hardwick Hall and written in the hand of James Wheldon, Hobbes's amanuensis and a servant of the Cavendishes, appears the listing "Caven., L. [sic]. *Horae Subsecivae*" (Hamilton 1978, 448, 451).[12] Further support for this attribution is an entry in the Stationer's Register for July 1, 1637, which notes "Lord Cauendishes Essaies" (Arber 1875–77, 4:362 [388]), but does not indicate to which Caven-

---

how the "Discourse on the Beginning of Tacitus," in particular, reveals this relationship between Hobbes and Machiavelli.

10 This is "A Discourse Against Flatterie," which is not included here since the wordprint analysis pointed to an author other than Hobbes for this work. The first reference to this discourse is as a 1611 book with the title *A Discourse against Flatterie;* it was published anonymously and is listed as no. 6906 in Pollard's catalogue (1946); Pollard attributes the volume to Grey Brydges, Lord Chandos, to whom the *Horae Subsecivae* had been attributed by some. This cannot be correct. Although this discourse was published anonymously, it is dedicated to the "Honorable Gentleman Lord Bruce, Baron of Kinloss." William, around the same time he became Hobbes's tutee in 1608, had married the twelve-year-old Christian Bruce, the only daughter of Lord Bruce. We may speculate that William dedicated this discourse to his new father-in-law. Jaggard's *Catalogue* of 1619 includes as entry no. 25.2, "Discourse against Flattery, by *William Cavendish,* Knight," but there appears to be no extant copy of this work (Willard 1914, 109). In what is undoubtedly the listing of the *Horae Subsecivae* in the Stationer's Register for March 29, 1620, the work, listed next to Blount's name, is referred to not by its title but as "A book called *A Discourse against Flattery,* and *of Rome* with Essaies" (Arber 1876, 3:311 [667]). This ties the *Horae Subsecivae* directly with the "Discourse against Flattery" attributed to William Cavendish the year before.

11 The former librarian at Chatsworth, Francis Thompson, notes that this inscription is written in the hand of the first earl of Devonshire and that he was the only one to call William, the second earl and Hobbes's first tutee, "Cavendysh."

12 The title without attribution appears in an earlier list of books in the library compiled in the late 1630s and written, according to Hamilton, in Hobbes's hand (1978, 446, 450). There is also a listing of "*A discourse agt Flattery,*" again without attribution.

dish this refers nor does it make clear whether it is a reference to the entire *Horae Subsecivae*. By the end of the seventeenth century, though, the *Horae Subsecivae* was attributed to the second earl's older brother, Gilbert, who died around 1614 at a young age.[13]

Horace Walpole (1806, 2:185) established the tradition for the eighteenth century that the *Horae Subsecivae* was the work of Grey Brydges, the fifth Lord Chandos, to whom it is often currently attributed (see above, note 7). This appears to be an attribution arising from an orthographic confusion between "Chandos" and "Candish," a variant of "Cavendish." Sir S. E. Brydges in his *Memoirs of the Peers of England* likewise names Chandos, arguing against the attribution of the book to Gilbert Cavendish by noting that "Gilbert appears to have died too young to have had the experience which it seems to contain" (1802, 1:385n) and not even suggesting that William was the author. Dissatisfaction with the Brydges attribution led at least one literary critic, at the beginning of the twentieth century, to argue on the basis of literary style and similarity of phrases that Francis Bacon was the real author of the work (O'Brian 1909).

All the speculation and claims suggest the interest that this work has aroused; now with the statistical authorship analysis, also called wordprint analysis, by Noel B. Reynolds and John L. Hilton (1993), we can assert at least that Hobbes is the author of three of the discourses, and affirm that the twelve essays and the longer "Discourse Against Flatterie" are written by someone else. This someone else is likely to be William, but we

---

13   See Wood ([1619], 1817, 3:1196); and Kennet (1708, 5), who wrote: "Gilbert ... died a young man of comparable parts, and left a very ingenious Book, entitled *Horae Subsecivae: Observations and Discourses*, &c." Thompson, the former librarian at Chatsworth, adds the following speculation to a memorandum attached to the "Essayes": "Kennet is likely to have been repeating a family tradition which may have had some foundation. Possibly Gilbert was the original author of the essays, but on his death they may have been taken over by his younger brother; while Hobbes may have been their real author." Thompson's suggestion that Hobbes wrote the "Essayes" is clearly incorrect according to wordprint analysis. Unfortunately, wordprint analysis cannot help us assess Gilbert's role in the production of the "Essayes."

have no known writings of Cavendish that would make it possible to verify such an assumption through wordprint analysis.[14] While the essays and the "Discourse against Flatterie" are clearly not written by Hobbes, they do fit well with each other, suggesting that the *Horae Subsecivae* may have been a compilation of the work of Hobbes and his tutee, a man the same age as Hobbes and with whom the relationship appears to have been more one of friends than master and servant (Aubrey 1898, 333). Such a collaboration might mean that the essays and the discourses that we cannot attribute to Hobbes could nevertheless give insight into Hobbes's interests and thoughts during this period. But while the essays and the discourse on flattery are ripe for such speculation, the three discourses by Hobbes which were also published by Mr. Blount for the reader's "contentment" give us a far more secure ground on which to analyze the early thought of Hobbes and assess the influences on it. Having these three discourses now enables us to explore the "tentative experiment" of the young Hobbes, the "eager period of search" that had previously gone "unreflected in his pages" (Oakeshott 1946, xiv).

PROOF OF AUTHORSHIP AND STATISTICAL WORDPRINT ANALYSIS

Over the last three decades scholars have developed a variety of techniques for performing statistical wordprint analyses of

14   There is some independent evidence of Cavendish's accomplishments; see the summary account of his long correspondence with Fulgenzio Micanzio, a friar in the service of the Venetian state and a confidant of Paolo Sarpi, in Reynolds and Hilton (1993, 362) and the detailed account of Gabrieli (1957). See below Part III, p. 128n. See also Hobbes's panegyric for William in his dedicatory epistle to his translation of Thucydides. William clearly had something of a checkered career, however, as Aubrey makes clear in his stories of the nature of Hobbes's service to William (1898, 1:328–30), and as an eighteenth-century biographer notes: "His house rather appeared like a Prince's court than a subject's and by his excessive gallantry and glorious way of living, he contracted a vast debt, and greatly impaired his fortune" (Grove 1764, 2). The *Dictionary of National Biography* notes ambiguously that he died in 1628 of an "excess of good living," leaving his family in a state of indigence. Hobbes left the service of the Cavendishes to accompany another young

disputed texts. The empirical discovery lying behind word-printing is that, just as individuals have distinctive fingerprints, so also their writings reflect consistent patterns in the usage of noncontextual terms.[15] These patterns are both idiosyncratic and statistically detectable. While the effectiveness of word-printing has been repeatedly demonstrated in controlled studies, there is not yet any consensus on a psycholinguistic theory that would explain the phenomenon of wordprints. Nor is there consensus on a single best statistical methodology for identifying the most distinctive word patterns.

Wordprint studies have proven useful in assessing competing theories about the authorship of such diverse texts as *The Federalist* and the Pauline epistles. The ability of modern computers to manipulate large texts has made it possible to perform increasingly sophisticated and statistically reliable analyses in more recent years. In the last decade, John L. Hilton and various associates, principally of Brigham Young University, have taken advantage of this increased computer power to develop statistical models that are more conservative in their assumptions and less aggressive in analysis than other popular models. Their concern has been to eliminate the risk of producing self-fulfilling prophecies.

We chose to use Hilton's model because of its conservative nature and our conclusion that it runs little risk of error. It also has the distinct advantage that its statistical calibrations are based on a large study of known English authors that serve well as controls for Hobbes and the *Horae Subsecivae*. Reynolds and Hilton undertook this study in 1988 and began publishing results in 1992.[16]

---

nobleman to the Continent before returning to Chatsworth in 1631. See also Saxonhouse (1981, 542–48).

15 Wordprinting studies tend to focus on what they call "noncontextual terms" because the patterns of usage for these terms do not tend to vary much as an author moves from one subject or genre to another or across the span of his writing career. In English writing, noncontextual terms usually include prepositions, pronouns, and conjunctions which do not change meaning or function in different contexts.

16 The findings were first discussed publicly in the April 1992 joint international meetings of the Association for Literary and Linguistic Computing and the Association for Computers in the Humanities at Christ Church, Oxford.

Outline of Wordprint Analysis Procedures

The main steps in this analysis include the following:

1. Blocks of typical text are selected, consisting of 4,998 words, exclusive of quotations and other elements that might skew the analysis. In this case we drew sample blocks from the writings of Hobbes, Bacon, Greville, our standard set of control authors, and the *Horae Subsecivae.*

2. Each block is scored in terms of all 65 of A. Q. Morton's noncontextual-word patterns.[17] Morton devised these measures specifically to be independent of vocabulary or style, and to be insensitive to changes of context or genre.

3. The 65 scores for each word block are compared statistically with the corresponding scores of every other word block. This produces a score for each combination of word blocks that consists in the number of the 65 patterns which measure a clear statistical difference between them.

4. In accordance with the control-author studies, pairs of blocks with seven or more different patterns are deemed to have different authors. Overall findings are summed and evaluated.

We used samples from most of Hobbes's English writings, and particularly those produced closest in time to the *Horae Subsecivae,* as listed at the end of this chapter. To obtain 4,998-word blocks in the *Horae Subsecivae* we had to lump ten of the shorter essays from the first part of the book into two blocks. The assumptions of this procedure seem to have been vindicated by results that show apparent author integrity within text blocks. However, significant statistical differences in word patterns suggest different authors for the larger group of essays on the one hand and the three discourses on the other. A third block was created using most of two remaining essays from the first part of the book. Each of the longer discourses in the second part of the book was divided into two text blocks.

An informal report followed soon thereafter in Noel B. Reynolds and John L. Hilton (1992). The final detailed report of the Hobbes-*Horae* study appears in Noel B. Reynolds and John L. Hilton (1993). This last publication elaborates a number of side issues that will not be reviewed in this volume.

17 See Part 4 for examples and more discussion—and Appendix 3 for the complete list.

As our primary external controls, we compared each of these texts to a standard set of writings selected from several known English authors by Hilton and Jenkins.[18] As additional external controls, we also prepared comparison texts from two other contemporary writers, Francis Bacon[19] and Fulke Greville. Bacon was selected because of the similarity of the essay style and the recurring speculation that he may even have authored the *Horae Subsecivae*. Greville was an associate of Bacon with comparable education.

Comparing Word Blocks
The next step is to compare each of the text blocks with all the others. This is accomplished by comparing each possible pair on each of the 65 noncontextual-word patterns and counting the number out of these 65 for which the two texts are statistically different.[20] This numerical score is recorded in table 1 for each of the compared text-block pairs.[21]

18   Hilton and Jenkins (1987) explain how their large study of known English authors provides the statistical benchmarks for their subsequent word-print studies.

19   The Bacon findings are reported in Reynolds and Hilton (1993), but not here. Because they proved to be nontypical for free-flowing, single-author prose, the Bacon texts were not suitable for use as a control in this study. This raises no problem for the Hobbes-*Horae* study inasmuch as we already had a large battery of control texts in place. It did, however, raise some intriguing questions about Bacon's writings, including the possibility that some of his secretaries who helped him in the early 1620s, especially Hobbes, might have been significantly involved in the composition process. These questions are now the subject of a further study.

The specific Bacon and Greville texts that were used for the first version of this study are listed in Appendix Two.

20   As is explained in Part IV below and in prior publications, this process is actually more complex than a single count. It is not the actual number of occurrences of each pattern that shows the significance of the comparison, but the mean calculated from 49 separate measurements of the patterns, where each count starts at a new (equidistant) place in the text. The multiple counting and wraparound partitioning significantly increase the statistical accuracy of the process, and complicate the calculation procedure.

Saying that two texts are statistically different on one of the word-pattern measures means the difference observed between them is too large to be explained by chance.

21   Because we actually make these comparisons 49 times, as explained in the preceding note, these scores are the median number of null-hypothesis

Table 1. Tabulation of Null-Hypothesis Rejections for All Combinations of the 59 Files of the Hobbes Study

```
               HOBBES              GREVILLE      HORAE             CONTROL AUTHORS                    CON.  F C   A
 T L L L L L L E E E E E E B B B   P P P P P P   C F F L R R T T E E                                 AUTH  I O   U
 H E E E E E E L L L L L L E E     R R R R R R   O L L A O O A A S S                                 MEAN  L D   T
 U V V V V V V A A A B B B H H H   1 1 1 2 2 2   U A A W M M C C S S   1 1 1 1  4 4  5 5 5 5  7 7           E E   H
 . . . . . . . . . . . . . . .     . . . . . .   . . . . . . . . . .   A B C D  A B  A B C D  A B
 1 1 2 3 4 5 6 1 2 3 1 3 4 1 2 5   1 2 3 1 2 3   1 1 2 1 1 2 1 2 1 2

 3 7 4 1 4 3 3 5 2 3 4 3 1 3 2    10 9 10 7 710  6 7 6 4 1 4 2 2 7 8    6 9 10 13 12 14  5 8 5 6  9 9    8.83 THU.1
   3 1 2 4 3 3 1 3 2 1 3 3 4 4     9 6 8 5 711  10 7 8 3 2 3 2 3 6 7    7 7 8 12 10 10  8 8 5 5  6 8    7.83 LEV.1
     2 3 1 4 3 3 5 4 0 4 4 5 6     5 7 6 4 6 6   7 3 3 5 5 3 4 3 6 8    8 8 8 9  9 7  7 6 3 7  7 9    7.33 LEV.2
       3 2 2 1 0 2 1 1 3 2 3 4     9 8 6 8 5 8   7 5 7 1 5 3 1 3 9 6   10 11 12 12 13 12  5 9 6 7  7 9    9.42 LEV.3
         1 0 1 2 2 2 1 3 2 3 2     8 6 8 6 4 8   5 3 5 1 1 2 2 2 5 6    7 6 11 9  8 8  3 6 3 3  7 8    6.58 LEV.4
           3 2 4 4 3 3 5 2 5 5     7 6 4 4 3 6   5 2 3 2 1 2 5 1 5 7    5 10 10 11 10 10  3 7 2 5  7 7    7.25 LEV.5
             2 3 2 1 1 3 3 6 3     8 4 8 5 5 6   7 4 6 4 2 4 4 3 6 7    8 11 10 14 11 13  4 8 4 6  9 9    8.92 LEV.6   H
               2 2 2 2 2 1 1 2    11 7 7 4 4 7   5 4 4 2 1 3 2 1 6 6    4 8 8 12  9 8  4 8 4 4  6 6    6.75 ELA.1   O
                 3 2 0 4 4 6 5    10 9 710 8 9   8 5 8 3 4 5 4 5 9 7   10 10 13 14 12 10  6 9 5 3  7 7    8.83 ELA.2   B
                   3 3 5 3 4 5     9 910 8 711   7 7 8 5 3 4 2 5 8 8    8 8 14 14 10 13  4 7 6 5  7 8    8.67 ELA.3   B
                     1 2 2 4 4    11 810 8 811   8 8 6 5 2 3 4 4 7 8    6 7 9 12 12 12  4 6 4 5  7 6    7.50 ELB.1   E
                       2 1 3 3     9 8 7 7 6 9   8 4 7 3 3 3 3 3 7 6    7 8 10 12 10 10  5 7 3 6 10 9    8.08 ELB.3   S
                         4 3 5    10 912 6 611   9 7 7 5 2 5 4 3 8 9    5 8 9 10  9 11  5 7 8 7  7 9    7.92 ELB.4
                           2 1     9 8 9 5 5 9   4 5 6 0 2 2 4 3 7 7    5 9 13 14 11 10  4 7 5 4  7 9    8.17 BEH.1
                             0     8 911 8 610   5 6 7 4 4 2 2 0 7 6    5 9 8 11 12 8  3 6 4 4  8 9    7.25 BEH.2
                                   7 7 8 5 2 8   5 6 8 2 1 3 2 3 7 7    7 10 12 12 13 10  3 9 6 6  9 12   9.08 BEH.5

                                   3 5 2 4 2    6 4 4 9 7 6 8 6 3 3    6 8 8 8  7 6  9 6 6 9  9 10    7.67 PR.1    G
                                     5 1 4 1    9 2 4 8 6 5 5 9 5 3    8 11 11 11 12 10  9 3 8 9  7 10    9.08 PR.2    R
                                       4 4 2    2 3 9 8 5 6 7 6 6 7   10 11 11 13 13 11  5 6 7 8  7 9    9.25 PR.3    E
                                         2 1    6 2 2 4 4 3 4 3 4 4    7 11 11 10 11 8  8 2 6 7  5 9    7.92 PR.1    V
                                           2    4 4 5 5 4 2 3 3 7 6    5 7 8 8  8 11  6 5 4 6  6 8    6.83 PR.2    I
                                                7 3 4 7 7 8 7 3 3    9 10 11 10  9 8  6 6 6 11 10 12   9.00 PR.3    L

                                                4 4 4 5 3 4 3 6 5    4 10 11 8 11 9  5 10 8 10 12 12   9.17 COU.1
                                                  2 2 4 4 5 2 4 1    6 10 9 13  8 8  6 6 1 8  9 11    7.92 FLA.1
                                                    4 5 4 5 2 4 2    6 10 12 13 11 10  7 4 5 12 12 12   9.50 FLA.2   H
                                                      3 1 3 2 9 4    6 12 13 14 12 12  7 7 3 7  8 8    9.08 LAW.1   O
                                                        1 1 2 5 4    5 5 10 9  9 10  2 6 1 4  4 6    5.92 ROM.1   R
                                                          2 1 4 5    4 9 10 11  9 9  4 4 5 3  6 7    6.75 ROM.2   A
                                                            1 4 5    5 8 6 9  9 8  5 8 4 5  5 7    6.58 TAC.1   E
                                                              1 4    4 6 7 9  7 6  5 5 1 8  6 8    6.00 TAC.2
                                                                2    6 8 6 8  8 5  4 3 4 10  5 8    6.25 ESS.1
                                                                     7 9 10 11  8 7  5 5 2 10  7 9    7.75 ESS.2

                                                                     3 6 4  5 7  5 5 4 8  8 8    6.25 -1A    C
                                                                       0 2  7 6  8 6 7 8  7 6    6.88 -1B    O
                                                                         2  4 3  8 8 6 12  8 9    7.25 -1C    N
                                                                            6 5  11 8 10 11  8 10    8.63 -1D    T
                                                                            2  10 10 7 11  10 10    8.00 -4A
                                                                               9 11 8 9  8 11    7.70 -4B
                                                                                 5 1 5  8 7    8.25 -5A    A
                                                                                 3 4  6 6    7.50 -5B    U
                                                                                 6 4        6.50 -5C    T
                                                                                 1 3        7.88 -5D    H
                                                                                      0     7.00 -7A
                                                                                           6.73 -7B
```

Authorship Testing of Specific Word Blocks

The fundamental assumption of wordprinting is that any single author's works will be relatively consistent between themselves in the frequency of specific noncontextual word-patterns they use, but that different authors will have significant differences. The norm established through the control-author study is that different authors always have a small number of null hypothesis rejections when their writings are compared, but that any one author will almost never exceed six rejections when any two blocks of his or her own works are compared. When tested against our diverse set of standard control texts, between-author comparisons average 8.26 rejections while within-author comparisons average only 2.58.

Figure 1 compares 16 Hobbes text blocks[22] to the control texts and shows just the kind of within-author and between-author separation we should expect when Hobbes is compared to the standardized control texts. It also shows our seventeenth-century control Greville, who looks like the rest of the control-author set when compared to Hobbes.

Wordprinting, Hobbes, and the *Horae Subsecivae*

The table displays two different patterns in the comparison between the *Horae Subsecivae* and Hobbes's writings. As shown in figure 2, none of the twelve *Horae Subsecivae* essays or the "Discourse on Flattery" match up well with Hobbes, though there is more overlap in some cases than would ordinarily be expected for texts by completely different authors. Our conclusion is that Hobbes cannot be the principal author of these texts, even if he may have had some influence as mentor or editor. Given the statistical design, we can be most confident of negative findings.

Our most important discovery is shown in figure 3. We find that none of the text blocks taken from the three long discourses on laws, Rome, and Tacitus has over five rejections in comparisons with each of the sixteen typical Hobbes texts.

---

rejections. For each of the 65 word patterns compared, the null hypothesis is that there will be no difference between the texts larger than would be expected from random normal variation. For each of the 65 which do have a larger than expected difference, the null hypothesis is rejected. For each set of comparison texts, the mean number of these rejections is calculated for the 49 countings and recorded as a score in our Table 1.

This table only includes the portions of the Reynolds-Hilton study that proved relevant for the specific findings reported in this volume. See Reynolds and Hilton (1993) for the full report.

22   Of the eighteen Hobbes text-blocks we analyzed, sixteen proved typical of his writings. See Reynolds and Hilton (1993) for details.

Figure 1. Distribution of Null-Hypothesis Rejections when Hobbes, Greville, and 12 Control Authors are compared to Hobbes

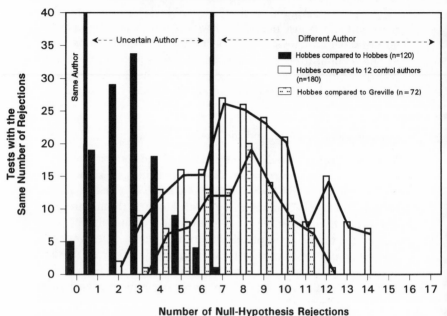

Number of Null-Hypothesis Rejections

As the individual and summary histograms show, these texts are statistically indistinguishable from uncontested Hobbes texts.

We cannot be sure that Hobbes did not write or help write some other small sections of the *Horae Subsecivae*. Most of the first ten essays are so short that had Hobbes written one or two only, we might not have picked it up in our analysis, which has bunched the ten of them together into two text blocks. We suspected at one point that the somewhat longer essay "On Religion" might be a Hobbes product. But intensive, customized testing of this essay alone demonstrated clearly that it is not typical of his writing (Reynolds and Hilton 1993, 367).

Figure 2. Distribution of Null-Hypothesis Refections when
the *Horae* Essays, "Against Flatterie," and "Of a Country Life"
are compared to Hobbes

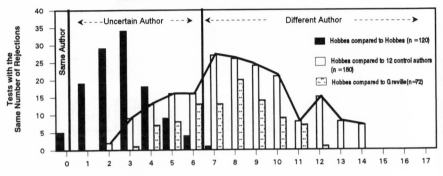

Horae Essays and Discourses that do not match Hobbe's wordprint

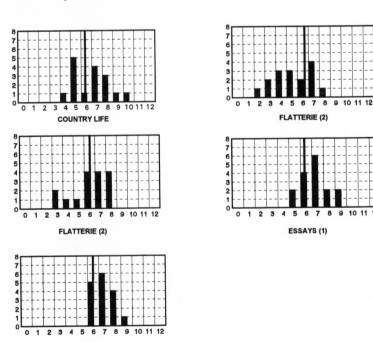

Figure 3. Distribution of Null-Hypothesis Rejections when the remaining *Horae* Discourses are compared to Hobbes.

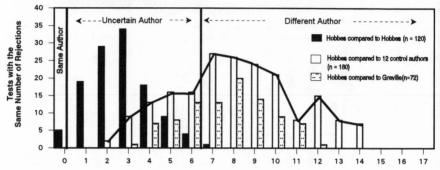

Horae Discourses that do match Hobbes's wordprint

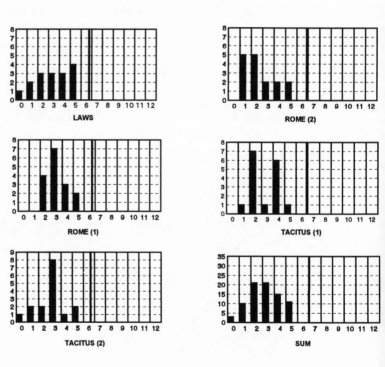

CONCLUSIONS

We have conducted an unusually large wordprint study to clarify the possible connection of the philosopher Thomas Hobbes to the *Horae Subsecivae,* a small volume of essays historically linked to Hobbes's only slightly younger tutee, William Cavendish. We found that the three long discourses that show up for the first time in connection with these essays in the 1620 edition definitely have noncontextual word-patterns identical to those in Hobbes's writings. However, the earlier materials, including the essays and the discourse on flattery, definitely do not share Hobbes's patterns, suggesting that even if Hobbes helped in their composition or provided some of the ideas, the final writing was done either by Cavendish himself or someone whom we have not considered. We have no historical reasons to discount Cavendish's authorship.

While the Reynolds-Hilton analysis refutes the broad hypothesis that the essays and discourses of the *Horae Subsecivae* may all have been written by Thomas Hobbes, its conclusions are substantially compatible with the earlier studies of the *Horae Subsecivae* by Saxonhouse.[23] Hobbesian influence must now be seen as absent or limited in the essays and the "Discourse Against Flatterie" to the possible influence of a tutor. We conclude, however, that Hobbes is the author of the other three discourses.

---

23 We cannot argue for compatibility with Wolf's findings, given his focus on the essays. See Saxonhouse (1981) in which she draws on her Yale dissertation (1972).

PART TWO

THREE
DISCOURSES BY
THOMAS HOBBES

THREE DISCOURSES
BY
THOMAS HOBBES

A NOTE ON
EDITING PRINCIPLES

Noel B. Reynolds

O UR OBJECTIVE in reprinting these discourses is to provide an accurate but easily readable text for contemporary students and scholars from a variety of disciplines. This has required modification of the 1620 text in conformity with the guidelines outlined below.

The pagination of the 1620 text is preserved by the insertion of original page numbers in square brackets immediately preceding the first complete word that appeared on that page. We did not think it important to show where original page breaks occurred in the middle of words. We use these numbers in our references to the text of the discourses.

We have usually maintained Hobbes's capitalization but have inserted missing capital letters at the beginning of sentences or questions in a series. We have usually modernized his spelling where the updating does not distort the nuances of the original. For instance, we replace *correspondency* with *correspondence, then* in comparative contexts for *than;* and *extirpate* becomes *extirpated. Is* becomes *are* where the modern ear requires the plural form. Relying principally on the *Oxford English Dictionary (OED),* we have provided notes explaining the usage of numerous obsolete words and words used in ways that might not be obvious to modern readers. It was interesting to note how often the *OED* uses examples from the *Horae Subsecivae* for early seventeenth-century usages.

When we have added to the text, we have shown such additions with brackets, as in "convulsion of the sinews in a natural [body]." Where those additions are modernizations of word usage, we have not included the brackets. Thus, we write "Some in this kind exceed others . . ." (*Rome*, 400), where the seventeenth-century *other* might look like an error to the modern reader.

We have followed the same principle of modernization in the Latin citations in the various essays. We have retained Hobbes's word order and his translations, which are often elegant but at other times painfully Latinate. Where Hobbes does not provide a translation of a cited passage, we have done so in the footnotes.

We have largely left Hobbes's punctuation alone, except for a small number of silent modernizations where the original punctuation would confuse or mislead the modern reader. There are a large number of sentence fragments that may bother the modern reader, but they could be eliminated only by altering the flow of Hobbes's text and by interpreting the text for readers. Hobbes's abbreviations are spelled out, as modern readers do not always have sufficient Latin background to know, for example, that Spur. Melius is Spurius Melius. We have also modernized the hyphenation, converting *vain-glorious* to *vainglorious*.

Possessives posed a particular difficulty because of the absence of apostrophes in the 1620 text. Distinguishing singular and plural possessives was almost impossible in some cases, such as Hobbes's descriptions of the *Popes palaces*. We have used context as a guide, but warn the reader that many such possessive constructions could be interpreted as singular or plural. We have also replaced the seventeenth-century conjunction of *his* and the proper name of the possessor with the conventional *'s* appended to the name.

The 1620 *Horae* uses italics in a way that is impossible to retain without causing confusion. We drop all the 1620 italicization of proper names. While we retain italicization for Latin quotations and terms, we drop it for Hobbes's translations of those quotations. We also convert his italicization of quotations (and paraphrases) in English into standard quotations with quotation marks. Again, the reader is warned not to expect all material in quotation marks to quote some source accurately. We also retain the italicization of Italian and other foreign-language terms. Finally, we drop Hobbes's frequent use of italics for emphasis.

INTRODUCTION
TO THE
Horae Subsecivae
by Edward Blount

To the Reader:

I take not upon me to write either in the praise, or discommendation of this Book; it belongs not unto me; but now it is abroad, must wholly be submitted to your judgment and censure. And I know, it must be the worth of a Book, and not the flourishing of an Epistle, that causes your approbation. So that this must stand, or fall in your opinion, by the weight or lightness that you shall find therein.

The Author of this Book I know not; but by chance hearing that a friend of mine had some such papers in his hand, and having heard them commended, I was curious to see and read them over; and in my opinion (which was also confirmed by others, judicious and learned) supposed if I could get the Copy, they would be welcome abroad. My friend's courtesy bestowed it freely upon me, and my endeavor to give you contentment, caused me to put it in print. And therefore to keep Decorum, and follow custom, in default of the Author's appearance, I present it to you with this short Epistle.

The Book, you see, is of mixed matter, by the way of observations, or Essays, and Discourses. There have been so many precedents of this kind, and (when they have come out of the hands of good Writers) always so approved, that there needs no Apology for putting in one Book, so different Arguments.

If the Observations, or Essays seem long to you, because most that have written in that way, have put them in less room; for that, if the fault grow by multiplicity of words, repetition, or affected variation of Phrases, then your dislike is well grounded. But when you have read, and find the length to have proceeded from the matter and variety, of it, I know, your opinion will easily alter.

I will hold you no longer from that, to which this but introduces: But if the Book please you, come home to my Shop, you shall have it bound ready to your hand, where in the meantime I expect you, and remain

At your command,
ED. Blount

A DISCOVRSE VPON THE BE-GINNING OF TACITVS.

His piece of *Tacitus*, which I make the foundation of this Difcourfe, and to which I haue here confined my felfe, containeth 1. The enumeration of the feuerall formes of the *Roman* gouernment. 2. The Authors digreffion touching the qualitié of one that is to

write

A DISCOURSE UPON THE
BEGINNING OF TACITUS

This piece of Tacitus, which I make the foundation of this Discourse, and to which I have here confined myself, contains: 1. The enumeration of the several forms of the Roman government. 2. The Author's digression touching the quality of one that is to [224] write a History. 3. The means Augustus used in acquiring and confirming to himself the supreme and Monarchical authority. 4. The providing for succession. 5. The plotting of Livia for the advancement of her children. 6. The estate[1] of the times after Augustus was fully settled. And lastly, the censure of such as (when Augustus began to grow weak and toward his end) might probably be thought to succeed him. And therefore in this order I begin with my Author.

Urbem Romam a principio Reges habuere [Tacitus, *Annales* Bk.1.1.1].[2] The City of Rome was at first governed by Kings.

The first form of government in any State is accidental: that is, according to the condition the Founder happens to be of. If one man of absolute power above the rest, be [225] the Founder of a City, he will likewise be the Ruler of the same; if a few, then a few will have the government; and if the multi-

---

1 State or condition; constitution or nature.
2 Subsequent citations from Tacitus almost always follow in order and will be cited parenthetically in the text by book, chapter, and line number only. The Latin has been revised according to modern conventions, although Hobbes's capitalization and word ordering have been retained.

tude, then commonly they will do the like. And it is but justice, for every man to have his own work subject to his own will. So here Romulus built, and ruled; was the founder, and was the King. The building of this City was about 800 years before the Nativity of Christ; and consequently from that time to this present, about 2420. The Contemporaries of Romulus reigning in Judah were Jotham; in Israel, Pekaiah; amongst the Medes, Artycas; in Macedonia, Thurimas; in Athens, Charops, who began the ten years government there instituted;[3] in Lacedaemon, Polidorus; and in Italy there were many petty [226] States, of might not much unequal, whereby this new City might the safelier grow up amongst them, and be the sooner able to match the most of them. For if any of those States had been of eminent power above the rest, it is likely, Rome should not have been suffered to have encroached so fast on her neighbors.

Now we have seen the times in which this City was built, let us next view how many Kings successively reigned over it, and how long this government continued. First, Romulus began, and there succeeded him, after one year's interregency, Numa Pompilius, then Tullus Hostilius, after him Ancas Martius, his successor was Tarquinius Priscus, next to him, Servius Tullius, and last of all, Tarquinius [227] Superbus. All whose reigns being gathered together, amount to the number of 240 years, and has been compared by Florus, to the infancy of a man, and commonly accounted the infancy of Rome, though I cannot find that they were much under the Rod,[4] till this last King's Reign, who, to his cost, found them already grown too stubborn. The next government of this State was Consulary.

Libertatem & Consulatum Lucius Brutus instituit [1.1.2]. Liberty and the Consulship Lucius Brutus brought in.

---

3 Charops is the name of a second century B.C. tyrant in Epirus who, like his grandfather with the same name, was pro-Roman. Perhaps it occurs here as a misspelling of Cecrops, the legendary founder of the Athenian monarchy (after Ogyges), who first divided the city into twelve town-districts. Athens was initially called Cecropia after him. Tacitus also cites one claim that Cecrops may have been the inventor of the shapes of sixteen letters to get the Greek alphabet started (*Annales* 11.14.8–10). Earlier sources also credit him with the introduction of monogamy and burial of the dead.

4 Suggesting they had not suffered tyrannical rule before this point.

Every one that has read the Roman Histories, can tell how much this act of Lucius Brutus has been magnified, insomuch as they instituted in the honor of it, an Holiday, by the name of *Regifugium:*[5] and how the [228] imitation of it drew another of the same race, and name, into such another action, who came not off with the like applause, though otherwise with the like fate. But I shall never think otherwise of it than thus: "*Prosperum et felix scelus virtus vocatur.*" [Prosperous and fortunate evil is called virtue.] For it was but a private wrong, and the fact not of the King, but the King's Son, that Lucretia was ravished. Howsoever, this, together with the pride, and tyranny of the King, gave color to his expulsion, and to the alteration of government. And this is by the Author entitled, Liberty, not because bondage is always joined to Monarchy; but where Kings abuse their places, tyrannize over their Subjects, and wink at all outrages, and abuses, committed against them by any either of their [229] children, or favorites, such usurpation over men's estates, and natures, many times breaks forth into attempts for liberty, and is hardly endured by man's nature, and passion, though reason and Religion teach us to bear the yoke. So that, it is not the government, but the abuse that makes the alteration be termed Liberty. This Consulary government began about *Anno Mundi* 3422[6] not long after the beginning of the second general Monarchy, which was of the Persians, amongst whom reigned Cambyses, Xerxes, and Artaxerxes, all within the space of fifty years, or thereabouts. And in the Athenian State lived Themistocles, and Aristides, in those days famous.

Now during this Consulary government, [230] there were others intermixed.

Dictaturae ad tempus sumebantur [1.1.2]. Dictators were chosen but upon occasion.

This Magistrate, for power, was limited only by his own will. For time, he had limits from the Senate, and those so short, that

5 Literally, flight or expulsion of the king, celebrated on February 24.
6 The *Anno Mundi* designation indicates years since the creation of the world in 4004 B.C. as calculated by Archbishop James Ussher, a contemporary of Hobbes.

their power could do little hurt, and bred little ambition. They had now authority like absolute Kings, and by and by had no more than a King in a Play. But when it came to the hands of such as could not easily be constrained to lay it down, they found it of that power, that by the color thereof the people were bereaved of their liberty, and enthralled to Sulla during pleasure, and to Caesar during life. But the Dictatorship is not to be accounted another form of government, but only an Office [231] in the Commonwealth, though for the time supreme.

Neque Decemviralis potestas ultra biennium [1.1.3]. The *Decemviri* passed not two years.

After the people had delivered themselves from the authority of Kings, and came themselves to undergo the cares of government, they grew perplexed at every inconvenience, and shifted from one form of government to another, and so to another, and then to the first again; like a man in a fever, that often turns to and fro in his bed, but finds himself without ease, and sick in every posture. They that could not endure one King, were soon weary of ten Tyrants, and for their extreme ambition, vexation, and cruelty, as also because of the licentious and barbarous lust of [232] Appius Claudius, one of the number, (who for the satisfying of his appetite, had judged a free woman to slavery) they soon extirpated that authority: but indeed the thing they most feared, was, that they saw those who possessed the power for the present, would not give it over, but sought to make it personal, and perpetuate it to themselves. They were jealous of their liberty, and knew not in whose hands to trust it, and were often at the point to lose it: but at this time licentious and inordinate lust gave them once more an occasion to shake off the yoke. As afore the Tarquins, so now the *Decemviri* suffer for the same offense. They for the ravishing of a Wife; these for the intended deflowering a Virgin: the first acted, and herself revenging it on herself by [233] her own hand; the second purposed, but prevented by a Father's hand, in the murder of his own Daughter. This alteration in government began 58 years after the expulsion of Kings, about *Anno Mundi* 3500. And 19 years after this time, began the Peloponnesian wars. In these times lived Pericles, Alcibiades, and Thucydides in the State of Athens.

> *Neque Tribunorum militum Consulare ius diu valuit* [1.1.3–4]. Neither did the Consulary authority in Tribunes of the Soldiers remain long in force.

After the Decemvirate, they returned again to Consuls: they were not long content with them, but bestowed the same authority on Tribunes of the soldiers; and weary of these, they had again recourse unto the Consulship. For the State [234] at that time being young and weak, loved change and variety of governments: but the emulation of the Commons, to equalize the Nobility, did give the principal occasion to these alterations. For on whomsoever the commons conferred the supreme authority, the Senate and Nobility still gained in all suits and offices to be preferred before them, which was the cause of most of the seditions and alterations of the State.

> *Non Cinnae, non Sullae longa dominatio* [1.1.4–5]. The domination of Cinna and Sulla did not long endure.

It is true that these men attained unto supreme power by violence and force, but yet I cannot think that to have been the cause why their power was so soon at an end. For though violence cannot last, yet the effects [235] of it may; and that which is gotten violently, may be afterwards possessed quietly, and constantly. For Augustus also took upon him the Monarchy by force, and yet he so settled it, as the State could never recover liberty. These took no order, and it may be, had no intention to reduce the State of the Commonwealth to a Monarchy, more than for their own times, else they might peradventure have found ways how to have mollified or extinguished the fiercer, allured the gentler sort, prepared the whole State to a future servitude, and what they had obtained by arms, have assured to themselves by politic provisions: which not doing, was the cause that their authority came the sooner to an end.

> [236] *Pompeii, Crassique potentia, cito in Caesarem* [1.1.5–6]. The power of Pompey and Crassus soon passed into Caesar.

This was an authority, in the Roman State, exercised without public permission only out of their own private strength. Of these Crassus was the most wealthy, Pompey the best beloved of the Senate, and Caesar of most power in the field. Their ambition was equal, but not their fortune, nor their wisdom. For Crassus was slain in the Parthian war, the which he undertook only out of avarice. Pompey, though he affected[7] the Monarchy, yet he took not the course that was fittest for it; for he then courted the State, when he knew his Rival had a purpose to use violence, and to ravish it. But Caesar knew the Republic to be [237] feminine, and that it would yield sooner to violence, than flattery; and therefore with all his power assaulted and overcame it: and so in him alone remained the strength of all the three till his death.

Likewise after the death of Julius Caesar,

Lepidi & Antonii arma in Augustum cessere [1.1.6–7]. The forces of Lepidus and Antonius came into the hands of Augustus.

This was the last change of the Roman government, and was permanent; for now Rome utterly lost her liberty. For Antony by occasion of Caesar's slaughter, being himself then Consul, having taken arms, which the State feared he would make use of to serve his own ambition, and to set himself up in Caesar's room:[8] the Senate gave authority to Augustus [238] to levy an Army, and make head[9] against him. Which he did, and within a while after agreeing with Antony, and taking Lepidus in for a stale,[10] established this Triumvirate, which in the end was also wholly reduced to Augustus. So that hence may appear, that it is a most dangerous oversight, to put Arms into such a man's hands for our defense, as may advance himself by converting them to our destruction. To which purpose the Fable is also applied of the Horse, who suffering a rider and the bit, for his

7 Aimed at or aspired to.
8 Office, position, authority.
9 Advance or press forward in opposition.
10 Decoy. This is a term derived from hawking. As the *OED* notes, it commonly referred to "A person or thing made use of as a means or tool for inducing some result, as a pretext for some action, or as a cover for sinister designs" (*OED* def.5).

assurance against the Hart that fed with him in the same pasture, could never after recover his former liberty.[11]

Qui cuncta discordiis civilibus fessa, nomine Principis sub imperium accepit [1.1.7–8]. Who when the whole State was [239] wearied with civil discords, received it under his government with the Title of Prince.

The manifold miseries that do accompany Civil Wars, and the extreme weakness which follows them, do commonly so deject[12] and expose a State to the prey of ambitious men, that if they lose not their liberty, it is only for want[13] of one that has the courage to take the advantage of their debility. And when a mighty and free people, is subdued to the tyranny of one man, it is for the most part after some long and bloody Civil War. For civil war is the worst thing that can happen to a State: wherein the height of their best hopes can come but to this, to venture and hazard their own, to overthrow their friends' and kindred's fortunes. And [240] they that are at the worst, have reason to be content with, and wish for any change whatsoever. This was one occasion which Augustus laid hold of to establish the Monarchy, they were weary, their strength abated, and their courages[14] foiled.[15] Yet he would not presently take unto him the Title belonging to Monarchy, especially not the name of King, but *nomine Principis sub imperium accepit* [received it under his government with the Title of Prince, 1.1.7–8]. Every man that has an office of command, though never so mean,[16] desires a name that may express the full virtue of his place, and most men receive as great content[17] from Title, as sub-

---

11   This is usually called the Fable of the Horse and the Stag (or Hart) and can be found collected in *Aesop's Fables*, V. S. Vernon Jones, trans. (New York: Avenel Books, 1912), p. 211.

12   To reduce the force or strength of, to weaken.

13   Lack or absence. While this usage will be familiar to most readers, it occurs so frequently in these essays that it may be worth clarifying once.

14   Used this way, the obsolete plural might mean intentions, purposes, or desires, as well as spirits or courage.

15   Defeated, overcome, trodden upon.

16   No matter how inferior in rank.

17   Hobbes's substantival use of *content* in the sense of satisfaction is frequent in these essays, but always a bit jarring to modern ears.

stance. Of this humor Augustus retained only thus much at this time, that he took a title which signified not authority, but dignity before all the rest: as if [241] the people of Rome had been to be numbered one by one, he thought himself worthy that they should begin with him. Also he knew that the multitude was not stirred to sedition so much, with extraordinary power, as insolent Titles, which might put them to consider of that power, and of the loss of their liberty. And therefore he would not at the first take any offensive Title, as that of King or Dictator, which for the abuses before done, were become odious to the people. And in a multitude, seeming things, rather than substantial, make impression. But having gotten the main thing that he aspired unto, to give them then content in words, which cost him neither money, nor labor, he thought no dear bargain. And [242] this was but for the present neither. For he doubted not but that the power which he had in substance, would in time dignify any name he should take above the name of King: and in the mean space [18] he should keep the love of the people, which is the principal pillar of a new sovereignty.

Hitherto, the several changes and alterations in the state of Rome, and how the sway thereof, after the space of almost 800 years, being now arrived at her greatest strength, remained wholly in the person of Augustus Caesar. He therefore after much deliberation had, whether he should restore it again to the former liberty of a Commonwealth, or convert the government into a Monarchy, at length resolved on the latter. The [243] means he had, and the devices he used to bring the same to pass, are now by the Author likewise touched, and should follow in order. But because Tacitus here digresses, to show the faults of Historiographers, and the uprightness he purposes to use in his own story, I will also take his words as they lie in my way, and afterwards proceed with the History itself.

Sed veteris populi Romani prospera vel adversa claris Scriptoribus memorata sunt [1.1.8]. But of the ancient people of Rome, both the

18 Meantime.

prosperous, and adverse estate has been recorded by re-
nowned Writers.

It is a sign of too much opinion, and self-conceit, to be a
follower in such an History, as has been already sufficiently
achieved by others. And therefore Cicero said well of the [244]
Commentaries which Caesar wrote of his own acts, and intended should be but the notes, and the ground of an History,
to be written by some that should afterward undertake that
task, that though that were an acceptable, and welcome work
to some arrogant persons, yet that all discreet men were
thereby deterred from writing. So, that as it was here to Tacitus, it should also be cause enough to any man else to abstain
from the writing of those Histories, which are already wisely,
and perfectly related. The reason why the times of the Commonwealth have been better Historified,[19] than those that
came after, seems to be the liberty that such a government af-
fords. For where the governor (who is always the main subject
of the [245] Annals of a City) is not one man but a great many,
there personal tax breeds not so often public offense.

Temporibusque Augusti dicendis non defuere decora ingenia, donec glis-
cente adulatione deterrerentur [1.9–11]. And there wanted not
good wits, to write Augustus's time, till by the prevailing of flattery they were deterred.

Also under Monarchs, so long as their deeds be such, as
they can be content to hear of again, the Historiographer has
encouragement to follow the truth in his writings; but when
they be otherwise, men must dissemble, if they will please, and
must please, if they will have their writings pass unsuppressed.
Therefore the known Law of History, which is *"Ne quid falsi*
dicere audeat, neque vere non audeat,"[20] that a [246] man should
not dare to say a falsity, nor not dare to speak the truth, must
needs be abrogated, where Flattery has admittance. For there

19 Celebrated, related, or recorded in history.
20 Hobbes appears to paraphrase Cicero, in *De Oratore* 2.62.5, who asks, *Nam*
quis nescit primam esse historiae legem, ne quid falsi dicere audeat? Deinde ne quid veri
non audeat? (For who does not know that the first law of history is that no
one should dare to speak falsely? Lastly that no one should not dare to speak
the truth).

it is more needful to have regard to the acceptance, than to the substance of our writings. And hereby Flattery in time comes to wear out, and consume the able writers in a Kingdom.

Tiberii, Gaiique, & Claudii, ac Neronis res florentibus ipsis ob metum falsae; postquam occiderant, recentibus odiis compositae sunt [1.1.11–13]. The occurrences of Tiberius, and Gaius, and Claudius, and Nero, whilst [they] themselves flourished, were for fear and after they were dead, out of fresh hatred, falsely written.

It is the condition of most men, having been restrained from moderate liberty in any thing whatsoever, when that [247] restraint is taken away, to become immoderate in the same. For their desires swell, and gather strength at the stop, which when it is removed, they run more violently than if they had never been hindered at all. Hence it is, that he which flatters during the danger, slanders when it is past, when the truth lies betwixt both: so that the same men that would before for fear most have blanched, are they that when they may do it safely, will most detract. And from hence it is, that the latter end of Augustus, together with the reigns of the four here named, had not as then found a faithful relator.

Inde consilium mihi pauca de Augusto & extrema tradere, mox Tiberii Principatum & cetera, sine ira, [248] *& Studio, quorum causas procul habeo* [1.1.14–16]. My purpose therefore is to deliver to posterity a few, and those the last things of Augustus, and then the principality of Tiberius, and the rest, without spleen, and partiality, the causes whereof are far from me.

The defects above mentioned, and want of a true History of these last times, caused the Author to take this task in hand, wherein to avoid the suspicion of the same faults he has before taxed in others, he puts in to our consideration that the causes both of spleen and affection, are far from him. These causes must be either fear, or hope, of future good or evil, or else some benefit, or injury formerly received, which every writer of History should do well to show himself void of, if he can; [249] because most men measuring others by themselves, are apt to think that all men will not only in this, but in all their actions more respect what conduces to the advancing of their own ends, than of truth, and the good of others. Thus much of the digression: now follows the History itself.

Postquam Bruto & Cassio caesis, nulla iam publica arma [1.2.1–2]. After that Brutus and Cassius being slain, the Commonwealth was no longer in arms.

Though Cremutius, that called Brutus and Cassius the last of the Romans, writing it in a time which would not permit a man so much as to look back at the former state of the Commonwealth, was perhaps worthily punished; yet this may be truly said of them, that they were the last Champions [250] of the Roman liberty. For after them no man ever bore Arms for Recuperation of that government. What an advancement then was it for Augustus that these were slain? For now the Commonwealth relinquished her liberty, and confessed herself subdued. So that his strongest adversary yielding, he might the more easily deal with the next.

Pompeius apud Siciliam, oppressus [1.2.2]. Pompey defeated in Sicily.

This Sextus Pompeius being the relics of the Pompeian faction, was defeated near Sicily, by Agrippa the Lieutenant of Augustus, in such manner, as of 350 sail,[21] he fled away only with 17. So that this was another step to the quiet establishing of his Empire. The first Civil war was between [251] the Caesarean faction on one side, and Pompey with the Republic on the other, and Caesar prevailed. The next will be a subdivision of the Caesareans, that Augustus standing on one part, and Antony on the other, the authority may at length settle in the individual person of Augustus, who hitherto has had to do against the faction of the Commonwealth and Pompey, in the wars against Brutus, and Cassius, and against Sextus Pompeius. How he will now divide from himself the other heads of his own faction, is next to follow.

Exuto Lepido, interfecto Antonio [1.2.2–3]. Lepidus being put out, and Antony slain.

21 Ships.

Lepidus if he had remained in the Triumvirate, might have hindered the contention of the other two, by keeping them in [252] doubt to whether[22] part he would incline. Wherefore, as if they desired to try the mastery between themselves, they won[23] Lepidus, whose authority was least of the three, to dismiss the Legions that were under his command, and to lay down his office. That done, the desire of sovereign rule would admit no longer friendship in the other two, so they fell to wars: and Augustus following it with all his power, brought Antony (who was already vanquished with effeminate passions, and had his heart chained to the delight of a woman) quickly to destruction, and himself remained sole heir of all their claims, and interests.

Ne Iulianis quidem partibus, nisi Caesar dux reliquus [1.2.3]. There remained not another Commander, no not in the [253] faction of Iulius but only Augustus Caesar.

This faction did not divide as long as Brutus and Cassius were alive, for then they had soon come to nothing, and the virtue of Brutus might have had as good fortune, for the maintenance of liberty, as that of his ancestor. But when they had made use one of another, to advance both of their hopes, then they parted, and contended who should be the sole gainer. Which happening to Augustus, he had afterwards no more to do, but only to keep what he had gotten; which he might easily do. For first he was alone, and when a man's power is singular, and his intentions are only of his own free election, he is then most likely to reduce them into act. Companions in such affairs [254] can seldom be content, that all counsels, nay almost that any, should tend to the other's profit; so constant is every man to his own ends. This Augustus foresaw, when he secluded from him those two, that were equal in authority and power with himself; Antony by force, and Lepidus by deceit. And now having power over the bodies of the people, he goes about to obtain it over their minds, and wills, which is both the noblest and surest command of all other.

22 Which.
23 Prevailed upon, induced, or persuaded.

Posito Triumviri nomine [1.2.4]. Laying away the name of a Triumvir.

He had three reasons to leave that Title; the first is of less weight, (except in Grammar) and that is the impropriety of that word applied to him that has charge alone, being proper only to such as be three [255] in Commission. The second is, because the name was too mean. For till this time, the Triumviri were rather for overseeing, than governing; sometimes appointed to look to one business, sometimes to another; but never had any whole charge of government of the Commonwealth, till such time as Augustus, Antony, and Lepidus, being three men, equally interested in the State, gave themselves that Title. But the chief cause was this, that the name carried with it a remembrance and relish of the civil wars, and proscriptions, which were hateful to the people. And a new Prince ought to avoid those names of authority, that rub upon the Subjects' wounds, and bring hatred, and envy, to such as use them.

[256] *Consulem se ferens, & ad tuendam plebem Tribunicio iure contentum* [1.2.4–5]. Calling himself Consul, and content with the authority of a Tribune to maintain the right of the Commons.

This officer of Tribune was ordained anciently, and so always continued, for a protector of the people, and a defender of their rights, immunities, and privileges against the violence, and encroachment of the Nobles. The authority therefore of this officer, together with the Title of Consul, Augustus took to himself, that even of the old offices he might have those, that were both for name, and effect, of greatest consequence. And for authority, there was none now greater than that of Tribune of the Commons. Insomuch as Tacitus says in another place,

Id summi fastigii vocabulum [257] *Augustus repperit, ne Regis aut Dictatoris nomen assumeret, ac tamen apellatione aliqua, cetera imperia praemineret* [3.56.3–6]. Augustus found out that name of chief dignity, that he might avoid the name of King, and Dictator, and yet have a Title of preeminence above other Magistrates.

But the main cause why he affected the Title of Tribune, was this, because he thought it best to make his faction sure with the Commons, who at that time were the strongest part of the

State, by having the Title and Authority of their Protector. And seeing it is impossible to please all men, it is therefore best for a new Prince to join himself to, and obtain the favor of that part in his State, which is most able to make resistance against him. This Augustus neglected not. But rather [258] used all means to draw all men to be contented with his present government.

Militem donis, Populum annona, cunctos dulcedine otii pellexit [1.2.5–6]. He allured the soldiers by largess, the people by provision of corn, and all men by the sweetness of ease, and repose.

Soldiers are most commonly needy, and next to valor, they think there cannot be a greater virtue than liberality, from which they think all Donatives proceed; when, if the truth were examined, it would appear that such gifts came not from the virtue Liberality, but were merely the price of their Country's liberty. But, this the Soldiers were too rude to examine. An open hand draws their affections more than any thing else whatsoever. The same [259] effect in the mind of the people is produced by provision of corn, which if they can buy at a lower price than formerly they could have done (though peradventure the measure be as much lessened as the price) they think then the State to be excellently governed. How effectual this kind of liberality has been, appeared long before this in the same State, when as Spurius Cassius, by distribution of money, and Spurius Melius, by largesse of Corn, were very near obtaining to themselves, an absolute sovereignty, and tyranny over the Commonwealth. This is also one of Augustus's designs. He steals the people's hearts by sustenance, and relief, as he did the Soldiers by his money. Further he pleases them [260] all with the sweetness of ease, and repose. They saw that to bear the yoke of Augustus, was to be freed of other vexation; and to resist, was to renew the miseries they were lately subject to. When they were much stronger, they could not make sufficient resistance, now they are weak, they can much less do it. Therefore being weary, they could not but be much won with the present ease, and vacancy of War, especially civil war. So Augustus took in this, the best order that can be, to assure a new sovereignty, which, is to afford the Soldier money, the People a good market, and all men ease, and quietness.

*Insurgere paulatim, munia Senatus, Magistratuum, legum in se trah-
ere* [1.2.6–8]. He began by degrees to [261] encroach, to assume the business, and charge of the Senate, of the Magistrates,
of the laws to himself.

Augustus had hitherto dealt with the State, as one that
tames wild horses; first, he did beat and weary them; next, took
care not to frighten them with shadows; then, showed them
hope of ease, and made provision of corn for them; and now
he begins gently to back[24] the State. He gets up by little and
little. For it is not wisdom for one that is to convert a free State
into a Monarchy, to take away all the show of their liberty at
one blow, and on a sudden make them feel servitude, without
first introducing into their minds some *previae dispositiones,* or
preparatives, whereby they may the better endure it. [262]
Hastiness in any action, especially of importance, is most times
the overthrow of it, and to do that at once, which must be done
successively, is an argument of a rash, and intemperate man,
that cannot contain himself, and stay for his desires. Also to a
people so long weaned from a Monarchical government, it was
most probable he might gain by degrees, insinuation, and continuance of time, more than on any sudden he could. Therefore he takes upon him the business, and charge of the Senate,
of the Magistrates, and of the Laws, and begins now to assume,
what he had long looked for, and expected. For whereas all
the plots and policies he had before used, [263] were to this
end, if he had not also come to fruition, he might have been
justly condemned of levity, and his actions to have proceeded
from a vainglorious, and unconstant brain, and his authority
would have in time come into contempt. For action and continual managing of business, is the only thing that preserves
the life, and vigor of authority. And all men give their respect,
and think it due to those, to whom they have recourse in the
dispatch of their weighty affairs.

Nullo adversante; cum ferocissimi per acies aut proscriptione cecidissent
[1.2.8–9]. No man now opposing him, the stoutest men being
fallen either in battle, or by proscriptions.

24 To mount a horse.

This encroaching on the liberty of the State, in former [264] times never wanted opposers: but now the stout Patriots were rooted out. For such men being forwardest, and busiest in Arms, must needs waste[25] sooner than the rest, and finding too much resistance, must therefore break, because they were of a nature unapt to bend. And again, in the proscriptions these only were they, that were aimed at, whereas the less violent adversaries found safety in contempt. The Prescription here spoken of, being that of the *Triumviri,* where the heads of the factions joining, abandoned, and as it were sacrificed their old friends to this new friendship, it could not be, that almost any stout, and dangerous man, of what faction so ever, should be left alive. And it may be it was no less advantageous [265] to the designs of Augustus, that some of his own faction were slain, than was the slaughter of those that took part with Anthony, and Lepidus. For they might have expected, for the requital of their service, to have been paid with participation of his authority, which he might not suffer, or else have grown averse, and have plucked him down, though they had with his fall crushed themselves to death. But Augustus was now rid of those stubborn companions.

> *Ceteri nobilium quanto quis servitio promptior, opibus, et honoribus, extollerentur; ac novis ex rebus aucti, tuta et praesentia, quam vetera & periculosa mallent* [1.2.9–12]. The rest of the Nobility, as any one of them was most ready to serve, so he was exalted to wealth [266] and honor, and being enriched by the change, liked rather the present State of things, and that which was safe, than the former, and that which was dangerous.

It is both justice, and good policy, to reward with preferments those that yield their obedience readily, and willingly; for it stirs emulation in men, to exceed each other in diligence. And on the contrary, to heap benefits on the sullen, and averse, out of hope to win their affection, is unjust and prejudicial. For first, they shall lose one benefit after another, through vain hope of winning them, and not losing the thanks of their first benefit; and then also others will learn, and think it wisdom to be averse and stubborn, by their example. Also those

---

25 To lose health, strength, or vitality.

that were rewarded for their service, must [267] needs strive to maintain the present State, and help to keep off the Civil wars. For times of tranquility be always best for the rich men. In wars and trouble they pay for all, and in desolation their loss is greatest. For Civil war is commodious[26] for none but desperate unthrifts,[27] that they may cut their Creditors' throats without fear of the gallows; men against whom the Law, and the sword of Justice makes a fearful war, in time of peace. But the rich, and such as were in love with titles of honor, found more ease and contentment here, than they could expect in the Civil war, and did accept the present with security, rather than strive for the old, with danger.

[268] *Neque Provinciae illum statum rerum abnuebant, suspecto Senatus populique imperio, ob certamina potentium, & avaritiam magistratuum; invalido legum auxilio, quae vi, ambitu, postremo pecunia turbabantur* [1.2.12–15]. Neither did the provinces dislike this state of things; for they mistrusted the government of the Senate and people, because of the contention of great men, and covetousness of the Magistrates; for the aid of the Laws was weak, being infringed by force, canvassing,[28] and lastly by money.

The Roman State did not consist in the magnitude of that one City of Rome, or in the extent of Italy alone, but in the multitude, and greatness of Provinces, that were subject unto it. And therefore it much concerned the surety of Augustus's government, to have also them content with this [269] alteration: which they were for two causes. First, a Popular State, if the great men grow once too mighty for the laws, is to the Provinces not as one, but many tyrants; so that not knowing to which faction to adhere, they procure the enmity always of some, and sometimes of all, and become subject to the rapine[29] of whosoever first seizes it, and to be the prize of their contention. At home they are commanded by contrary factions,

---

26 Advantageous.

27 Unthrifty, shiftless, or dissolute persons; spendthrifts, prodigals.

28 To solicit votes or support before an election. The Latin *ambitus* clearly indicates reliance on illegal and corrupt methods in this process.

29 Plunder, pillage, or robbery.

contrary Acts, so that they can neither obey, nor disobey without offense: but are hurried, and haled,[30] sometimes to this faction, and sometimes to that. Those that were deputed to do justice amongst them, must not administer the same according to the Law, but according to the humor of him, who himself [270] follows; which may be now one, and anon (fortune changing) another. At Rome, if they sued for any thing, though they could all be content their suit should pass for the matter itself; yet the furtherance that one faction should give it, would stir up contradiction in the other, and so cross it. Therefore it is better for a Province to be subject to one, though an evil master, than to a potent, if factious, Republic. Next, they found covetousness in the Magistrates. For when they expected, that having truth, and equity on their sides, their causes and suits should not go amiss, they found contrarily, that by that, their judgments were not balanced, but that they distributed justice rather by weight than measure. [271] That purse that was heaviest, that bribe that was greatest, carried the cause. Justice was not seen, but felt; a good bribe was their best Advocate. Such in those times were the Magistrates, and Judges. Every thing was carried by might, ambition, and corruption. He that was not ambitious, was neglected: and he that was not corrupt, was esteemed indiscreet.[31] In this time the Provinces would have been content with a Monarchy, or tyranny, rather than to be troubled with so different, and ill humors of divers[32] men. But there may also be covetousness in Magistrates, when one has the sovereignty, being a fault of the person, and not of the form of the government. Indeed, there may be bribing in such a State; but in a factious, and divided [272] Commonwealth it cannot be otherwise. For where the State is united, the Magistrates will have some respect unto that; but being divided, every one is for himself, and must look to strengthen and enrich himself by any means how ill soever.

---

30 Constrained or drawn forcibly.

31 Modern usage may mislead here. Hobbes is probably suggesting imprudence or lack of judgment in the conduct of one's life, and not just in speech.

32 In these essays Hobbes invariably uses *divers* as a synonym for *many, sundry,* or *several*—indicating some vague or undetermined number. In some contexts he could possibly mean *different,* in which case the text would need to be rendered *diverse,* as the use of *divers* in this way is now obsolete.

For faction has no strength, but from Injustice, and Rapine. One remedy there is for such an inconvenience, and that is, if the Laws be strengthened with authority; which also wanted in the former times. For force, friends, and money overthrew their validity. For what Law was so strong, that the force of Cinna, Sulla, Marius, Julius Caesar, and others, in their times could not have broken through? Nothing is more proverbial than that Laws are like Spiders' webs, only to hold the smaller [273] Flies. Then, favor and friendship, made way even for the weak men to break through. And lastly, money gave the easiest passage of all. Wherefore the Provinces, conceiving better hope of the rule of Augustus, could not dislike, but were rather glad of the alteration. Thus far the acquist[33] and assurance of the Monarchy to Augustus: now, his ways to perpetuate the same, and derive it to posterity, are to be considered.

Augustus subsidia dominationi Claudium Marcellum, sororis filium, admodum adulescentem, Pontificatu & curuli Aedilitate extulit [1.3.1–4]. Augustus, to strengthen his government, prefers Claudius Marcellus, his Sister's son, one as yet very young, to the Pontifical dignity, and office of Aedile.

A Prince that has raised [274] himself to the Sovereignty of a State, and is once quietly settled in it, will for the most part have a desire to make the same successive, and will take all opportunities that may further such his intention. So Augustus does now, and adorns with offices, and dignities, all those upon whom, he thought, he might make the Empire to descend. Provision of successors, in the lifetime of a Prince (besides that it is a kind of duty they owe their Country, thereby to prevent civil discord) has this virtue, that it nips in the head, and kills the seeds of ambitious, and traitorous hopes in those that think of alteration: whereas the uncertainty of the successor, breeds, and feeds Treason in aspirers for many years together. If any man therefore had [275] any hope alive in him, that when Augustus should die, the State might again struggle for liberty, or a new form of government might arise better to their own liking, this providence of Augustus does utterly extinguish it. First therefore, he puts his Nephew into these two places of

33 The act of acquiring.

great command, that of Pontifex, and the Aedileship: whereof the former, in matters of their Heathenish religion, was of supreme authority. In places of authority, and subordinate command, it is no small policy in the supreme governors, and especially in the principal offices, to place such as are either tied in nature, or necessity unto them: that as they themselves have supremacy in command, so all their underministers may be so fast unto [276] them, that their actions may be always limited according to the will, and affection of their Sovereign, by whom they were installed, and ordained for that purpose, to the places they hold. This was one stay and strength of his government, to put into the hands of his Nephew (as I may so say) the Supremacy in matters Ecclesiastical, which is one of the chiefest guides of a Commonwealth.

Marcum Agrippam ignobilem loco, bonum militia, & victoriae socium geminatis Consulatibus extulit [1.3.3–4]. He makes Marcus Agrippa, one descended meanly, but a good Soldier, and companion with him in his victories, twice together Consul.

After he had advanced his Nephew, the next that he exalts to dignity, was his friend. Wherein [277] we may perceive, that in the opinion of Augustus, when a Prince has a Minister of valor, and worth, which may make him capable of great place, the meanness of his birth ought to be no bar to his rising. Again, in raising him, first he should not need to fear that he might endanger him, being one that could presume so little of his Nobility. For a man that by his virtue raises himself from out of the common people, shall more often get envy from the multitude, than any popular applause, and consequently cannot be very dangerous. So Augustus conferred that honor safely. Besides, Agrippa, in that he was a good Soldier, deserved to have the reward of his virtue, which is honor. And lastly, as the companion of his Victories, [278] he deserved to participate of some fruit thereof. Which Augustus might also consider, not so much for his company in the war, as in the Victory. For men reward the success of actions done on their behalves, rather than the labor, and virtue, or the danger which they expose themselves unto in the same. The office of Consul was a great place, and had been in former times of supreme power in the Commonwealth: yet Agrippa being a man, of whose faith, love, and worth, he had had long experience, and for the reasons before recited, he doubted not to bestow the same upon him twice together: and more than that, intends to make him another stay, and hope of the succession.

Mox defuncto Marcello generum [279] *sumpsit* [1.3.4–5]. Shortly after when Marcellus was dead, he makes him his son-in-law.

The greatness of this benefit, bestowed on one that could no ways exact, or extort it from Augustus gives here an occasion to enquire into the minds of all men in the matter of giving and receiving benefits. Tacitus in the first book of his Histories, says, "*Beneficia eo usque esse laeta, dum exolvi possunt.*"[34] That benefits received are pleasing so long as they be requitable.[35] When once they exceed that, they are an intolerable burden, and men seldom are willing to acknowledge them; for who but a man of desperate estate will set his hand to such an obligation, as he knows he never can discharge? This is the reason that Princes are so slow in advancing some men, that have deserved it; [280] because they cannot easily do it according to their full merit, or else they think it will not be so taken: So that they should, by rewarding them, both pay, and yet remain in debt. And generally all men, but Princes most of all, hate acknowledgement, and like not to have such great Creditors in their eye; but will rather be content to take advantage against them, as against so many upbraiders of ingratitude: So that great services procure many times rather the hatred than the love of him they are done unto. On the contrary, when men can, without lessening of themselves, reward those to whom they have been beholden, so as to satisfy them according to their own estimate, they will then overdo it, and heap one favor [281] upon another, thinking by showing their affection to them, to gain theirs in the same proportion: but it falls not so out in human nature; for benefits increase the love of the bestower, more than of him that receives them: for as it

34 Hobbes mistakenly cites the *Histories*, but it is in *Annales* 4.18.11–12, that Tacitus states: "*Nam beneficia eo usque laeta sunt dum videntur exolvi posse. . . .*" In many such references Hobbes seems to be quoting from memory, without checking the original source.
35 Capable of being repaid or rewarded.

is "*proprium humani ingenii odisse quem laeseris* [Tacitus, *Agricola* 42.4.1–2]" the property of human nature, to hate those they have wronged; so also is it on the contrary, to love those to whom they have been beneficial. Agrippa had done great service to Augustus; but Augustus was now able, without diminution of himself, both to requite and surmount him; and therefore leaves out nothing that may express his gratitude, but makes him his Son-in-Law, whereby his children might become heirs even to Augustus's [282] own power, which was the absolute sovereignty of the whole Empire. Which act of Augustus, as it proceeded out of affection, so it also agreed with good policy; for whom should he more trust, than one whose love had been so much showed, whose fidelity so much tried? And therefore he sets him near himself, and (Marcellus being now dead) bestows on him the widow Julia, his only child.

But here I must have leave to transpose these few lines of the Author, to the end that that which touches the advancement of the children of Livia, may afterwards be joined together.

After this, he advances the Children that Agrippa had by this match.

> *Genitos Agrippa, Gaium,* [283] *& Lucium, in familiam Caesarum induxerat, necdum posita puerili praetexta, principes iuventutis, appellari, destinari Consules, specie recusantis, flagrantissime cupiverat* [1.3.7–10]. He received Gaius and Lucius, the children of Agrippa, unto the Caesarean family, and seeming to refuse, most ardently desired to have them, while they were yet but boys, to be called Princes of the youth and to be designed for the Consulship.

His sister's son Marcellus being dead, and having now of his own offspring to succeed him, he desires that the people would be pleased to take notice of them betimes, and in his lifetime, to put them into some possession of their future dignity. He would therefore now, whilst they were in their minority, have them honored first with the title of [284] Princes of youth. This title, did imply as much as Heirs apparent of the Empire. And to give it, was to admit and openly consent, that the State should be, not only the possession of Augustus, for his own life, but also the inheritance of his descendants forever. Secondly, with being Consuls elect, that they might have some command of importance, as soon as their age could bear it. Though Augustus had force to bring this to pass, yet he was loath again to irritate the minds of his new subjects; and therefore he would not openly so much as make show of this his desire touching his Grandsons, lest they who were content to obey him for his own time, upon this offering them a Successor, as the perpetuation of their servitude, might turn desperate, [285] and do some such act as might displease him. But he turns to dissimulation, which was in those times held an inseparable accident[36] of a politic Prince. He makes show of refusing, and yet most ardently desires it; and that desire must also appear by the refusal. And those that saw him thus refuse, dared do no other than force his consent, and put these honors on his Grandsons, whether he would, or not.

Tiberium Neronem & Claudium Drusum privignos Imperatoriis nominibus auxit, integra etiam dum domo sua [1.3.5–7]. And his own house not yet failing, he adorns with imperial titles Tiberius Nero, and Claudius Drusus, his wife's[37] children.

Augustus, to make the succession certain, and not to have it depend [286] upon the lives only of two, and those but young, advances also the sons of his wife, men of mature years, and seen in the wars, and honored them with imperial titles, that if his own issue failed, he might leave a successor, such as his own affection should make choice of. This course in the general, is to be esteemed in a Prince both a provident one for himself, and also in a manner necessary for the public good of his subjects, considering the bloody and fearful wars, that have followed upon the death of such as have not provided a successor before their decease. But yet it falls out otherwise in some particulars, than according to the intention of him that so nominates his successor; as it did in this: for had Augustus [287] thought it should so much have prejudiced his own

36 This could indicate a necessary quality or characteristic, though by 1846 J. S. Mill in his *Logic* is using this exact phrase to refer to universal qualities which are not necessary or essential.

37 Both here and later the original text uses the plural *wives*. But both references seem clearly directed at Augustus's second wife, Livia.

blood, to advance those of his wife,[38] he would I think have left them in obscurity. Therefore it is not good for a Prince in appointing his successors, to leave the reversion of the State to such as may have power and means to subvert the first heirs thereof. Thus far he has been tying the knot of succession, which now Livia his wife begins on one part to untie, or rather cut asunder, for the strengthening of the other.

Ut Agrippa vita concessit, Lucium Caesarem euntem ad Hispanienses exercitus, Gaium remeantem Armenia, et vulnere invalidum, mors fato propera, vel novercae Liviae dolus abstulit [1.3.10–13]. As soon as Agrippa was dead, Lucius Caesar going to take [288] charge of the Army in Spain, and Gaius coming from Armenia, untimely Death by fate, or else by the treachery of their Stepmother Livia, took away.

As the watchfulness of a faithful, and wise Counselor about a Prince, often checks the very thoughts towards treason; so on the contrary, the death of such a one wonderfully facilitates the designs of a traitor. When Agrippa was dead, his sons did not long outlive him, and though Tacitus here does not accuse Livia directly of their death, yet there may be gathered these presumptions against her. First, her ambitious and plotting humor. Then their hasty and opportune death; as if fate, (if their death were merely natural) had been of Counsel with her. And lastly, the benefit [289] which thereby accrued unto her own sons. This last is of much importance in the judgment of men: for to whomsoever comes the profit of strange and unexpected accidents, to him also, for the most part, is imputed the contriving, and effecting of them, if they be thought able. To Livia appertains the suspicion of their death, because it was good for her that they should die when they did, and she was also generally suspected in that kind of evil.

Druso pridem extincto, Nero solus e privignis erat [1.3.13–14]. Drusus being before dead, Nero was only left of his sons-in-Law.

This was the fruit reaped by the death of Augustus's Grandsons, for hereby her son Nero remained the only man that was likely to succeed in [290] the Empire. For his brother

38 See previous note.

Drusus died of a fall from his horse two years before. So that now he had no competitor neither of his own kindred, nor of the house of Augustus to oppose him, save only Agrippa Posthumus, who for causes hereafter to be mentioned, was not of much respect.

Illuc cuncta vergere, filius, Collega Imperii, Consors Tribuniciae potes-
tatis adsumitur, omnesque per exercitus ostentari, non obscuris ut antea
matris artibus, sed palam hortatu [1.3.14–17]. All inclined that
way, he is made his son, his Colleague in the Empire, his companion in the Tribunitial[39] power, shown to all the Armies, not
by the secret artifice of his Mother, as before, but by open persuasion.

Every man that followed Augustus in his [291] strength,
now in the declining of his age turn their eyes upon the next
change: for those who had fortunes under Augustus, desired
the conservation of them at the hand of the next; and those
that had none, began now to hope for estates and honors, under his Successor. All men being of this condition, that desire
and hope of good more affects them than fruition: for this
induces satiety; but hope is a whetstone to men's desires, and
will not suffer them to languish. It was wisdom in Augustus
to make manifest one certain successor, thereby not to give
occasion to the ambition of many. But that Tiberius should be
the man rather than his own Grandson, that was certainly the
wisdom of his Wife: for not many [292] men would deprive
their own offspring of so fair an inheritance, without greater
cause than is expressed, to confer it on the issue of another. If
Livia had loved her own no better, the house of Caesar might
have continued much longer than it did. The honor Augustus
gave to her son, was to adopt him for his; which was to give
him sole power for the future, after the death of Augustus, and
make him Colleague of the Empire, and partaker of the authority of Tribune, which was authority equal to his own for
the present; and then, to cause the armies to yield him their
respect, and acknowledge him for their next Lord. These favors Livia had been long soliciting for, by insinuation, [293]
detraction, deceit, and whatsoever Art else is requisite to the

39 Of or pertaining to a Roman tribune.

supplanting of a Rival in a Prince's affection. But now the way was so clear, by reason of the Emperor's age fit to be wrought on, and the rudeness of Agrippa, that she dared openly move Augustus to disinherit his own issue, and prefer hers. But the favor that Livia showed to Augustus's children, besides the suspicion of causing the death of two of them, was clean[40] contrary.

Nam senem Augustum adeo devinxerat, uti nepotem unicum Agrippam Posthumum in Insulam Planasium proieceret [1.3.17–19]. For she had so tied unto her Augustus, who was now an old man, that he confined his only Grandson Agrippa Posthumus into the island Planasia.

I have [294] not found so great a defect in Augustus's judgment, in all his former actions, as in this, so far to follow her will, as to banish and confine his own blood, for the advancement of hers. But, as Tacitus says, he was now grown old, and so the weakness that accompanies old age may excuse that fault, which in his younger, and more mature judgment, peradventure he would never have committed. It was hard for him, being now in years, to want the comfort of his Wife; to live with her, and not to have her pleased, intolerable, and against the dignity of an Emperor; and to extinguish her ambition, impossible. So that if he had seen her drifts,[41] unless they had broken out into some violent actions, he must in a manner have been forced [295] to dissemble it. For it is contrary to the dignity of a Prince, to take notice of that fault which he is not able to amend. But he saw them not: for what cannot the craft of some wives, through opportunity, continual flattery, and arguments framed with all the Art that can be used, work upon the weak judgment of an old man? The place of Agrippa's exile, being a small, and uninhabited Island, where he was rather imprisoned, than banished, was in a manner, a sure argument, that he should not long outlive his Grandfather: for as the fear of Augustus kept him now alive, so the fear of his own Title, would make Tiberius never let him escape out of his fingers.

40   Entirely, absolutely.
41   Schemes or plots.

Rudem sane bonarum artium, & robore corporis stolide ferocem, nullius [296] *tamen flagitii Conpertum* [1.3.19–21]. Ignorant (to say the truth) of good Arts, and bearing himself foolishly fierce of his strength of body, but not detected of any crime.

These are the causes, for which Agrippa was put by[42] the right of his succession, and wanted the respect which was otherwise due unto his birth. He had not good education. That was the sum of all his faults. And in a State which might freely elect their Prince, the same had been a just cause to pass by him. For it is a great misfortune to a people, to come under the government of such a one, as knows not how to govern himself. For where it is said, he was unfurnished of good Arts, it is not meant of letters, though that also be good in a Prince, and of ornaments the chief; for he [297] may want these, rather than judgment, valor, or goodness of nature. But the Art that he is principally taxed to want, seems to have been the Art of conforming to times, and places, and persons, and consists much in a temperate conversation, and ability upon just cause, to contain and dissemble his passions, and purposes; and this was then thought the chief Art of government. And whereas he is said to be undetected of any crime, that made not much for the matter in hand; for though he might prove no ill man, he might be nevertheless an ill governor. But Agrippa's defects were not the sole cause of his disinheriting, though they were the sole justification of it, when it was done. The hope of succession, notwithstanding the [298] care of the Emperor, being reduced by the Art of Livia, to one only man, Augustus again takes order for the bringing in of one more.

At hercule Germanicum Druso ortum, octo apud Rhenum legionibus inposuit, adscirique per adoptionem a Tiberio iussit, quamquam esset in domo Tiberii Filius iuvenis; sed quo pluribus munimentis insisteret [1.3.21–24]. But yet he made Germanicus the son of Drusus, Commander of eight Legions upon the Rhine, and commanded Tiberius to adopt him, although Tiberius had a young son of his own; but this he did, to have the more supports.

42 Prevented from attaining.

Augustus is still of this judgment, that the succession ought not to depend on the life of one man, and therefore will have more props to establish it. But as the advancing [299] of Tiberius, was thought to be the ruin of Gaius, and Lucius: so now the making of Tiberius to adopt Germanicus, might have proved the ruin of Tiberius, if the Ambition of Germanicus had been answerable to his power. For Augustus put eight Legions into his hand, the which afterwards would not only have been ready to have given him the Empire, but also went about to put it upon him by force. Therefore if a Prince raise many to the hope of reigning, he ought to provide against the emulation, ambition, and mutual jealousies that ordinarily arise thereof. For else he shall hardly bring any of them to the fruition, or if one, then all the rest to untimely ends. Augustus here gave Livia indeed no occasion to work against this last choice [300] of his, being one of her own Grandchildren; but yet to command Tiberius, who had a son of his own, to adopt another, must needs breed a heart-burning[43] in him, because he knew by himself, how much rather men desire to possess, than expect such authority. And fearing therefore, that Germanicus might bear the same mind, he afterwards, as is thought, took a course to bring him to his end, whereby may be perceived in what danger an honest man stands, being near unto one that is ambitious, either before or behind him, whose nature is to destroy before him, out of hope; and behind him, out of fear.

After that Augustus had mastered, quieted, and taken order for the succession of the Empire: the Author [301] shows next the state of the present times. And first for matter of wars abroad.

Bellum ea tempestate nullum, nisi adversus Germanos supererat: abolendae magis infamiae ob amissum cum Quintilio Varo exercitum, quam cupiditate proferendi Imperii, aut dignum ob praemium [1.3.25–28]. There remained at that time no war, saving against the Germans, and that rather to wipe off the disgrace for the loss of the Army with Quintilius Varus, than out of any desire to enlarge the Empire, or hope of worthy recompense.

43 Jealousy, discontent, grudge.

Wars are necessary only where they are just, and just only in case of defense. First, of our lives, secondly, of our right, and lastly, of our honor. As for enlargement of Empire, or hope of gain, they have been held just causes of war by such only, as prefer the Law of [302] State before the Law of God. But this war against the Germans, was to defend the reputation of the Roman Empire, and was necessary, not for the curiosity[44] alone, and niceness,[45] that great Personages have always had, in point of honor, much more great States, and most of all that of Rome, but also for the real and substantial damage (for some man might account the other but a shadow) that might ensue upon the neglecting of such shadows. For oftentimes Kingdoms are better strengthened and defended by military reputation, than they are by the power of their Armies. For there is no man that does an injury to another, and escapes with it, but will attribute his impunity to want of power in his adversary, (for there be few that [303] want will to revenge disgraces) and thereby be the more emboldened to do him another, and so another, as long as they may patiently be endured; whereas, when they deal with one whose sword is out at every contempt, they will be very wary not to do him wrong. And besides this, Augustus might find commodity[46] in this war, by employing therein the great and active spirits, which else might have made themselves work at home, to the prejudice of his authority.

> *Domi res tranquillae. Eadem Magistratuum vocabula. Iuniores post Actiacam victoriam, etiam senes inter bella civium nati. Quotus quisque qui Rempublicam vidisset* [1.3.28–30]? In the City all was in quietness, the same names of Magistrates. The younger sort were all born after the victory at Actium, [304] and even the old men in the time of the civil war. How few were left that had seen the Commonwealth?

After the violent storms of civil wars, succeeds now the calm of Augustus's government. For it fares with the body of a whole State, as it does with the body of one man, that when a

---

44 Carefulness or exactness.
45 Fastidiousness or exactness.
46 Advantage.

Fever has spent the matter, and bilious humor, whereby itself was nourished, the body comes afterwards to a moderate temper.[47] Whatsoever might have caused a desire of returning to their former liberty, and bred a grudging of the old disease, was now removed. Few remained that had seen the ancient Republic. And there is never in men so strong a desire of things they have not seen, as of those things which they have. And a man's nature is to stir [305] more for the recovery of a good, which they once enjoyed, than for the acquisition of what they are ignorant of. As for the longing which might arise in them, through relation, and report, they had therein also some satisfaction. For whereas they might have heard of the names of Consuls, Tribunes, Censors, and the like, the same they found also in the present State; though the authority of them all, remained only in Augustus.

> *Igitur verso civitatis statu, nihil usquam prisci & integri moris: omnes exuta aequalitate, iussa Principis aspectare* [1.4.1–2]. So that the State of the City being changed, nothing remained of the old, and uncorrupted customs, every one (equality laid of) attended the commandment of the Prince.
>
> *In vita hominum perinde accidit, ut si ludas* [306] *tesseris etc.*.Terentius.[48] It falls out in a man's life, as in a game at Tables, wherein when one cannot cast that which is the best, he must mend the matter as well as he can, by good play.

The change being now fully settled, and the ancient customs no more hoped for, they find, that striving for equality, is not the best of their game, but obedience, and waiting on the command of him that had power to raise, or keep them low at his pleasure. For though other virtues, especially deep wisdom, great, and extraordinary valor, be excellent ones under any sort of government, and chiefly in a free State, (where therefore they thrive best, because they are commonly accompanied with ambition, and rewarded with honor) yet in the [307] subject of a Monarch, obedience is the greatest virtue, and those before mentioned as they shall serve more, or less unto that, so to be had more or less in estimation. Therefore they now

47 Balance of the humors in the body.
48 This is loosely quoted from Terence's *The Brothers* 739.

study no more the Art of commanding, which had been heretofore necessary for any Roman Gentleman, when the rule of
the whole might come to all of them in their turns; but apply
themselves wholly to the Arts of service, whereof obsequiousness is the chief, and is so long to be accounted laudable, as it
may be distinguished from Flattery, and profitable, whilst it
turn not into tediousness.

Nulla in praesens formidine, dum Augustus aetate validus, seque, &
domum, & pacem sustentavit [1.4.3–4]. There being at that time
no fear of troubles [308] as long as Augustus undecayed by age,
sustained both himself and his house, and the Public peace.

Although that the principal strength required, to the managing of an Empire, be that of the mind, yet ability of the body
is also of such necessity, that without it a Prince runs the danger of suffering many disorders that he would else remedy. The
cause hereof is obvious to every man, namely, that when for
weakness of age, or want of health, he cannot be present at the
consultations of those he uses in matters of estate, he must be
forced to rely on the relations of divers,[49] and so be subject to
distraction,[50] or else wholly trust unto some one, and become
liable to abuse. And in the meantime every great man, hoping
to [309] make his private benefit out of the public remissness,
severally oppresses the common people, and withal, keep off
their complaints from the Prince's ear; and thereby draw on
the danger of sedition and rebellion.

Postquam provecta iam senectus, aegro & corpore fatigabatur, ader-
atque finis & spes novae: pauci bona libertatis in cassum disserere,
plures bellum pavescere, alii cupere, pars multo maxima inminentes
dominos variis rumoribus differebant [1.4.4–8]. But now that he
was grown very aged, and wearied with his sickly body, and that
his end and new hopes were near at hand: some few there were
that discoursed in vain of the commodities of liberty, more
feared war, some desired it, but the greatest number by far, with
diversity of rumors did descant[51] on those that were to be their
next [310] Lords.

49 Reports of others. See above, note 32.
50 Confusion or disorder caused by dissension or internal conflict.
51 Comment or discourse on, criticize.

When a Prince draws near to his end the people's minds are all set upon new hopes, and discourse of nothing that is present, but only of what is in expectancy. The reason hereof is this, the hopes of Subjects being much built upon the life of their Prince: when he dies, they are of necessity to begin again, and lay their foundation anew in the next. Augustus therefore being ready to leave his room to another, there could not choose but be much discourse of the probability of the successor. One of these three was of necessity to come in place: Liberty, Civil war, or a new Monarch. If another Monarch then either Agrippa, or Tiberius. For Liberty they had no hope at all, but yet that was also talked of: for men have generally [311] this infirmity, that when they would fall into consideration of their hopes; they mistake, and enter into a fruitless discourse of their wishes; such impression do pleasing things make in man's imagination. As for war, it was both feared, and desired by many, according as their fortunes required it; for without doubt, those whose estates were whole, would be afraid, though such as had not a fortune able to sustain their inordinate expense, thereby to seize the wealth of other men, would much wish for it. Lastly, touching a Monarch, as it was most credible to come to pass, so which of the two it should be, was now become the common talk of the greatest part of men, who censuring their persons, gathered arguments thence of their [312] succession, and of the welfare of the estate under them; and used liberty in their speech of them, more boldly (though nevertheless privately) than in the times that came next after, they could safely have done. Thus far the state of those times, wherein Augustus was come to the last Scene, and ready to quit the Stage of this great Empire. And now Tacitus comes to the opinion conceived of those that were next to enter.

Trucem Agrippam, atque ignominia accensum, non aetate, neque rerum experientia tantae moli parem [1.4.8–10]. That Agrippa was cruel, and kindled with his disgrace, and neither of age, nor experience sufficient for so great a burden.

By the weight of these censures, I should hardly think they proceeded from the common [313] people, but rather that they sprung out of the Author's own meditation, or else that he means by "*pars multo maxima*" the greatest part of the Nobility, and men of knowledge in great affairs. Age and experience are necessary for the government of a great Empire; therefore the want of these in Agrippa, was of much importance against him; so also was the fierceness of his disposition, the absence of which fault is more desired by subjects in their Prince, than of any other vice whatsoever, that concerns only morality. But that other note given to Agrippa, that he was "*ignominia accensus*" [kindled with his disgrace], is a far greater exception against him than all the rest. The great men had most of them no doubt approved his banishment, and he lived thereby [314] in contempt of them all; so that he could not choose but hold himself generally injured, though his ignominy proceeded but from a few: and opinion of contempt is a frequent cause of cruelty and tyranny. If now therefore they had chosen him for their Prince, they had then given him full power to make his revenge according to his own cruel inclination, and done contrary to the custom of human nature; for men more willingly trust him with their lives and fortunes, that has done them injury, than one that has been or holds himself injured by them: for from these they can expect nothing but revenge, from the other they may hope for amends. But this is not always the best course, considering on the other side another [315] general disposition of mankind, which is apter to remit to such as are under their power an injury received, than to make satisfaction to them for one committed; because for the first they shall have thanks, and the second is held but for a debt.

After the censure of Agrippa, falls in that of Tiberius.

Tiberium Neronem maturum annis, spectatum bello, sed vetere atque insita Claudiae familiae superbia, multaque indicia saevitiae, quamquam premantur erumpere [1.4.10–13]. That Tiberius Nero was of ripe years, and of reputation in the wars, but he had in him the old and hereditary pride of the Claudian family and many signs of cruelty broke forth in him, though he strove to smother them.

Ability to govern is not all that is to be wished for in a Governor; Tiberius was [316] here thought too able, that is, likely to hold the reins of government too hard, especially over a people so lately weaned from liberty: for such are ever more sensible of every restraint and pressure of Monarchical rule, than others are that have been so accustomed. There are not two more tyrannical qualities in the world than pride and cruelty; whereof the former imposes intolerable commands, and the latter exacts immoderate punishments. They argued Tiberius's pride both from his ancestors and education, and of cruelty [he] himself made demonstration. Men derive their virtues and vices from their ancestors two ways; either by nature or imitation. By the former are derived all that depend on the temper of the body; the rest are by imitation, [317] and do seldom fail. For the reverence that naturally men do bear to the qualities of their ancestors, begets a lively imitation of them, in their posterity. And so pride may pass through a Stock by imitation, not that men would imitate that, but by error under the name of Magnanimity. Then for his cruelty, by how much the more he endeavored to hide it, and could not, by so much the more it was feared and abhorred in him. For a passion that can be mastered, is nothing so dangerous as one that cannot, especially in Tiberius, that knew best of all men how to dissemble his vices. Those things that Tiberius would dissemble, were evil, and those evils he could not dissemble, were great ones; therefore for such cruelty as [he] himself was not able to cover, he [318] was justly to be feared. And yet it is no easy thing to dissemble one's vices, I mean, if the dissimulation must be of long continuance; for, for once a man may overcome the most violent passion that ever was: but "*difficile fictam ferre personam diu*" (Seneca, *Tragedies*).[52]

Hunc & prima ab infantia eductum in domo regnatrice; congestos iuveni consulatus, triumphos [1.4.13–14]. That the same man was brought up from his infancy in the house of Sovereignty; that he had Consulships, and triumphs heaped on him while he was yet but a youth.

This is another argument of the haughtiness of Tiberius, drawn from his education. Honors sometimes be of great power, to change a man's manners and behavior into the

52 Hobbes notes that this quote comes from Seneca's *Tragedies*. It is certainly found in *De Clementia*, where he says: *Nemo enim potest personam diu ferre, ficta cito in naturam suam recidunt* (1.1.6–7).

worse, because men commonly measure their own virtues, rather by the acceptance that their persons find in [319] the world, than[53] by the judgment which their own conscience makes of them, and never do, or think they never need to examine those things in themselves, which have once found approbation abroad, and for which they have received honor. Also honor many times confirms in men that intention wherewith they did those things which gained honor; which intention is as often vicious as virtuous. For there is almost no civil action, but may proceed as well from evil as from good; they are the circumstances of it (which be only in the mind, and consequently not seen and honored) that make virtue. Out of all these things, I suppose, may be gathered, that honor nourishes in light[54] and vain men a wrong opinion of their own worth, and consequently, often changes their manners into the [320] worse, but especially that it increases their pride and insolence. As for his education in a house of sovereignty, that might put into the heads of these censuring subjects thus much: (for certainly they liked never a jot the better of Tiberius for having been brought up in so high a School of sovereignty as the house of Augustus). First, that what seeds soever of haughtiness and pride were in him hereditary, and which he possessed by virtue of his blood, were now also through long custom sprung up, and wanted but the season of reigning to bring forth their unpleasant fruit. Secondly, that having by experience, under so learned a master in the Art of government been taught how to hold them under as much as [he] himself should please, they could not look for any remissness [321] to proceed from want of knowledge how to keep them low, and consequently were sure to find his government every way uneasy.

Ne iis quidem annis quibus Rhodi specie secessus exulem egerit, aliquid quam iram, & simulationem, & secretas libidines meditatum [1.4.15–17]. Neither those years that he lived under color of retirement in exile at Rhodes, did he meditate anything but wrath, dissimulation, and secret lust.

53 The text reads "them," apparently a misprint for "then," which we have frequently corrected to our modern "than."
54 Not commanding respect.

It is reported of Tiberius, that at the first he travelled voluntarily to Rhodes, but being there, he was commanded to stay. Howsoever it was, he obtained the fair name of retirement, to cover the ignominy of banishment. A man would perhaps think, that adversity should rather quench, or at least assuage those passions, which have their life [322] especially from great prosperity, as wrath, and dissimulation, and lust. And so it does, when the adversity is so great, that the hope is lost of reducing their meditations into act. But otherwise it works a clean contrary effect. For whereas anger commonly dies, where revenge is despaired of; dissembling is laid aside, where the labor of it is vain; and imaginations of lust diminish, where they can never be accomplished; when adversity is but such as they expect to overcome, it often falls out, that the hope which nourishes such imaginations is inflamed thereby, and men please their vicious fancies for the present, with the conceit of what they will execute with effect hereafter, when they shall have the power. This was the case of Tiberius, and a cause of fear, and censure in those that [323] were to live in subjection under him.

> *Accedere matrem muliebri impotentia: serviendum feminae, & duobus insuper adulescentibus, qui Rempublicam interim premant, quandoque distrahant* [1.4.17–19]. That besides this, there was his mother of feminine impotence: that they were to serve a woman and two young men, that would for the present oppress the Commonwealth, and might hereafter rend it.

Next to the person of Tiberius, they considered in him those of his Family, that would also look for service, and obedience at their hands, namely, his Mother and two sons: Germanicus by adoption, and his own natural son, and thought them no small grievance to the Commonwealth. For it is a hard matter to serve and please well one Master: but to please two, or more, when there is, or may be, betwixt [324] them competition, or jealousy (leaving out that one of them is a woman) is altogether impossible. The cause hereof is not, because the diligence and dexterity of a man cannot suffice for the quantity of service, but because the quality of it will not permit: for the service that the one will expect from you, is most times this, That you displease the other. And this proceeds from the emu-

lation of those that are in the way to authority, that often labor
not so much to outrun each other in the course, as they do to
trip up one another's heels. And the same emulation, when
they once draw near the race's end, makes them snatch at the
prize, and fall to violence, and war, and to distract, and draw
the Commonwealth into faction and sedition.

FINIS.

A
DISCOVRSE
OF ROME.

IN the fight of any place there bee two especial Obiects, *Antiquitie*, and *Greatneſſe*, both which none can fooner challenge then *Rome*: in the very beginning noted for *Soueraignty*. The continuance of which, in fuch diuerfity of gouernments, as *Kings*, *Conſuls*, *Tribunes*, *Dictators*, *Emperors*, cannot but fhew a diuine power; for

Z 2   other-

A Discourse of Rome

[325] In the sight of any place there be two special Objects, Antiquities, and Greatness, both which none can sooner challenge[1] than Rome: in the very beginning noted for Sovereignty. The continuance of which, in such diversity of governments, as Kings, Consuls, Tribunes, Dictators, Emperors, cannot but show a divine power; for [326] otherwise so many changes might in all likelihood have bred confusion, and so consequently suppressed their rising to so great an Empire: which as the last, so it may be truly styled the greatest that yet the world ever knew, or heard of; obtained only by the valor of this one City, no Commander, and for a long time no Soldier, that came not out from thence. So that it may be said, the people of this one place, made themselves masters of the rest. Whereupon they might have just cause to esteem *Orbem in urbe,* the world confined in their City.

In the height of whose Imperiality, which was in Augustus's reign, Christ came into the world. This as then the chief Commandress of the whole, was the place where [327] holiness, and religion, aimed to have their principal plantation; where, during the time of the infidelity of the Emperors, till Constantine the great, who was the first that maintained the faith, it is infinite to comprehend the tyrannizing over Christians, the martyrdoms they endured, so many, that it is hard to name any who sealed not his faith with his blood.

1   Claim.

71

But now Constantine was converted, to see the ill effects so good a cause produced, cannot but breed admiration. For the Ambition of the Bishops of Rome made this their first step to greatness, and subversion of the Empire. How grounded upon this donation,[2] I cannot imagine, nor I think they yet well defend: but this was the true Original [328] by which in succession of time the Empire was translated.[3] The zeal of this, and some succeeding Emperors, was so well taken hold of by the Prelates of Rome, that by degrees they assumed more authority to themselves than was due; the other in a manner before they were aware losing all at Rome but the title. From which pretended power, the Popes now take to themselves supremacy in all causes, through all Kingdoms in the world, and those which were before, their superiors, to be as it were subject, and created by them that were their creatures. Which shows a great contrariety to the pretended arguments of Romanists, for superiority, and rather may be returned upon them, that this their greatness has more risen by encroachment [329] than right. Why therefore Princes have been so blinded with their pretenses for greatness, I cannot tell whereunto to attribute it, except to the fate of this place, that has ever been, or aimed to be the Mistress of the world. First, by their wisdom and power, and then under color of Religion and Saint Peter's Keys.

And now to the description of Rome, as I saw it. In which I will neither go beyond mine own knowledge, and fly to the reports of others, nor yet so strictly tie myself to a bare description, but that I may upon the occasions of those particulars I saw, set down my observations, and the conceits[4] I then had, which consist, first in the situation. Secondly, the Ethnic[5] [330] Antiquities. Thirdly, the Christian Monuments. Fourthly, the

2 The reference is to the Donation of Constantine, the forged document in which Constantine was purported to have conferred on Pope Sylvester (314–35) extended dominions and political and judicial authority. It was enormously influential from its first invocation in 1054 until it was exposed as a forgery in the fifteenth century.

3 To convey or remove from one person to another.

4 Conceptions.

5 Pagan.

modern Buildings, Gardens, Fountains, etc. Fifthly, the Colleges, Churches, and Religious Houses. Sixthly, the present strength of the City and Pope, with the description of his and the Cardinals' Magnificence. And lastly, the safety and danger for an English man to travel to Rome.

If you observe the situation, it stands in a place that could neither afford pleasure nor profit to the dwellers, other than that which is forced. Though not so seated, as it may be said to stand in the Appenine, yet amongst those Mountains. All the Country about is so barren, except some little, near the City, which is by labor brought to fertility, that the wildest Forest [331] of England may be esteemed good ground, in respect of this. In some places hereabout, I saw where corn had been gathered, but by the stubble might perceive had been so thin, that a man would think one stalk had been afraid of another. The ways thereabout both coming down the Appenine to Rome, and from thence toward Naples, so unpassable for a Coach, that a man may think himself well blest, if he break not his neck from horseback.

The sight of this so miserable a Country, wonderfully distracted my thoughts, to think how the inhabitants of so wild a place could ever come to such a greatness. And from thence proceeded these cogitations. First, that ease and delicacy of life is the bane of [332] noble actions, and wise counsels. A man that is delighted and whose affections be taken with the place wherein he lives, is most commonly unapt, or unwilling to be drawn to any change, and so consequently unfit for any enterprise, that may either advance his own honor, or the good of his Country. Any actions that reach farther than their own private contents, in their estimation be needless and unprofitable Labors. And it has many times happened, that whilst men live in this Lethargy, that Countries, Cities, their own fortunes and all, have been lost through their negligence.

Again, a life of pleasure does so besot and benumb the [333] senses, and so far effeminate the spirits of men, that though they be naturally prone to an active life, yet custom has brought them to such a habit, that they apprehend not any thing farther than the compass of their own affections; think nothing beyond their present enjoyments. A strange Epicurean opinion, that men, who were born to have dominion over all creatures, should be now subject to them, and under their rule. A mere inversion of the prime ordinance.[6]

From this consideration I declined to the contrary, that a place of hardness, and a life exercised in actions of valor and not idleness, has ever produced the bravest men, and arrived at the greatest fortune. [334] Let but the Roman Story be a mirror to you in this kind, you shall hardly, I think, find in the first times any enterprise of great worth, that the cause of it might not be drawn from this head. For their first poverty, being men brought to this place by fortune, and rather by forced, than desired election, not knowing where else to settle, in despite of[7] want, their ambitions put them forward; first, to encroach upon their neighbors, and then, as their fortunes were enlarged, to go on in actions of greater consequence and more difficulty. Being a race of such men, as could not confine and limit themselves to one place, but successively from father to son, you shall scarce read of any, that was not either [335] a man of action or direction, though some peradventure naturally unapt for the one, yet exquisite in the other: and ability to give counsel, is at least , not inferior to the former.

To prepare a man fit for both, nothing so much prevails, as a hard and weary life, such an agitation as will not permit idleness, nor the mind to settle too much upon private ends, which being so, could never be aptly applied for Public [ends]. Besides, a continual working of the mind, which in an active spirit, will still grow and labor in production of good effects, if it should be suffered to rest, would soon degenerate. For if a man give over himself to an easeful life, the sharpness of his senses will be dulled, and grow retired, [336] applying himself to his own contents, and then, can never have sufficiency, nor will to prevail for the public, once being confined to his own particular interest, and looking no further. Many men are naturally given to such a life, and some by accident fall into it, but certainly their memory dies with them: for no man is born only for himself. This is so well known, that I will not seek farther to illustrate it.

6 An allusion to the dominion given to Adam in Genesis 1:26.
7 In spite of.

A third consideration that came into my mind, at the sight of the place, was to wonder at a sort of men (but either ignorant, or malicious) who from the spirit of detraction think to calumniate, the valors, and virtues of men, in disgracing their Country for barrenness, for poverty, or the like. These [337] men, if they had ever seen this place, and known the story, would never have imagined this a good argument. Cannot virtue and poverty be together? Cannot an unfruitful Country yield men full of worthiness, and Valor? A strange mark of an envious disposition, to tax the men's virtues, for the unpleasantness of the soil; as if virtue and plenty could not be severed, or that of necessity a hard Country must produce soft and ignoble spirits: but if they would truly look into themselves, they could not choose but see a wonderful imperfection, and ignorance, who judge virtue by means, and men by places. If Noble and worthy Spirits had consisted in these outward respects, the men of this place would have been wonderful [338] ignominious; but you may plainly see, by the example of them, that a poor and hard life, a desolate, and almost uninhabitable place, brought forth such men, and they performed such actions, as in this age (we are most of us so much degenerate) we can hardly hear of without incredulity. So I will leave the place itself, and speak of the Country about it.

Not far distant from the City, is the Mediterranean Sea, and the principal Port now is *Civita vecchia*, where since the Church has had dominion, the Navy is very small, and chiefly consists of Galleys. But certainly, this was a great help, in the time of the ancient Romans, as well to increase their dominion, as to fortify themselves against foreign invasions: for by [339] this means men were more easily, and with less charge transported to those parts of Africa, and Greece, where they made great conquests, which otherwise could never have been compassed, and they themselves much strengthened against all enemies that could come from those parts, seeing it a matter of great difficulty to surprise, or take any place, that has so good a defense as the Sea. And to a people who be strong, and of great power, it is not difficult to defend themselves from the enterprise of any assailers; and experience has ever shown, it is harder to conquer Islands and places well fenced with the Sea, than the Continent.

Thus much for this, and now I will confine myself within the walls, which be the ancient ones, [340] adorned in former times with many towers, but now the most decayed, and not very many left. The River Tiber runs through the town, and within this compass are those seven Hills so famously known, all of one side the River, upon which old Rome was built. And still there be some Palaces on them; but the City, as it is now, is more built in those spaces, as *Campus Martius,* etc. which before were left vacant.

But I will now take a view of the ancient Antiquities, and first, of the famous Capitol upon one of the seven Hills, called *Mons Capitolinus,* whereof almost nothing remains but the memory. The place where the Senate sat, is now plain, and covered with earth, only some steps you may see where they went [341] down, and it is said to have been framed in the form of a Cockpit.[8] The houses now about the Capitol are assigned for the place of Justice. Three several[9] ascents there be by stairs unto it; and I have heard those Romans, who are descended from the Ancient, do (though at any price) desire to have their dwelling hereabouts. The principal of them be of the Scipioni, and the Camilli. From this place Nero made a Gallery to his Palace upon *Mons Palatinus,* whereof there is now nothing remaining, but some few Pillars which bore it up, very great ones, and of Marble. This place is adorned with many choice Statues, both in the open place, and buildings about it. In the open place you shall see a Statue, lying upon a Marble stone in a fountain, called [342] Marforius, (*Pasquins Intelligencer*). There is also the Statue of Marcus Aurelius in brass, and upon horseback, not anciently here, but removed hither from a more obscure place, by Paul III, Pontifex Maximus.[10] Besides, there is the Statue of a woman Comedian, represented as if she were speaking, and two Auditors listening unto her, so lively expressed, that a man not instructed, may easily know they were made for this representation. In the

8 An enclosed area in which gamecocks are set to fight for sport.
9 Separate.
10 This is the only extant equestrian bronze surviving from ancient Rome. Its survival may be due to the fact that it was mistakenly thought to represent Constantine.

buildings there be also many principal Statues, as one of a Scolding Woman, so well done, as it would almost fear[11] one to look on it. A Hercules in Brass. Julius and Augustus Caesar in Marble. Romulus and Remus sucking a Wolf, in Brass. Quintus Curtius on horseback, in brass, and Jupiter in Marble. Of [343] Romulus and Remus sucking a Wolf there be many in Rome, and not defaced, being ever left by them that sacked it, to put the people in mind of their base beginning. But it seems, in this respect, they never thought the worse of themselves, seeing they have in so many public places made representation of this. There is besides, the Statue of Nero's Mother, wherein her countenance of sorrow is expressed, when the news of her son's unnaturalness[12] meant to her was told. There is another in brass, of a Boy, taking a thorn out of his foot, looking so earnestly, and pitifully, that a man would think he had some sense of pain. There be in this place many other Antiquities of this kind, which to avoid prolixity, I omit to name.

[344] Descending from the Capitol, there be three or four Triumphant Arches dedicated to the honor of Emperors, as to Augustus Caesar and Constantine, where be engraven their principal Acts, and victories: but the most remarkable of these, is Vespasian's erected upon his return from Jerusalem, where you shall see the overcoming of the City, lively set forth, and the holy things which he brought away from thence in triumph, as the Candlesticks and the rest singularly expressed. Here is also the great Amphitheater, but now extremely ruinate, where the most public shows and sports were usually shown. Upon *Mons Palatinus,* where Nero's magnificent house was built, there is nothing to be seen but decays, and now [345] employed to [13] a Vineyard, which is bestowed upon the English College. At the foot of the farther part of this hill is the place, where, upon great Feasts, the Naval Battles were wont to be presented. Not far from thence is the Pantheon or Rotunda, in *Campo Martio,* a place built round and high: at the

11   Frighten.
12   Unnatural conduct or disposition. The term often occurs in reference to crimes or sins against family members.
13   Used as.

entrance are many Marble pillars of great thickness, and height, having one only light in the top like a Louver.[14] This anciently was a Temple dedicated to all the Gods, and now converted to the honor of all Saints. The two Pillars that be erected as Triumphs to Trajan and Antoninus, are of a great height, and exquisitely engraven upon the sides, with their acts and victories. Upon the top of Trajan's, his ashes are said to be in a [346] ball of gold. In the house of Alfonso Suderetti, is the place where Caesar made his Tomb, whereof now almost nothing remains but the ruins: this he purposed not only for himself, but his Family; it is a great compass, built round, and some old pieces of the Tomb yet remain. In many places of this City, there are to be seen the ruins of the ancient Emperors' Baths; amongst which, the most principal are those of Diocletian, of a wonderful great compass. Upon this, it is said, that for twelve years together, multitudes of Christians were condemned to continual working. Some part of it now is converted to a Church and Monastery. Without *Porta Pinciana,* there is the Temple of Bacchus, which stands upon Marble pillars, [347] and it is a fair Rotunda. Here his Sepulcher is set about with pillars, and the tomb itself is of Porphyry curiously[15] graven. This temple, is now divided into two parts, and dedicated to two Saints, Saint Agnes and Saint Constanza, whose bodies have been there lately found, and that of Saint Agnes is said to be uncorrupt. This Temple was of late all covered with earth, and but newly discovered. By *Porta Ostia* there is a Tomb of one Cestius an Aedile, which was an ancient office amongst the Romans, principally to look to burials. This is built in manner of a Pyramid, all of great and broad Marble half in the wall and half out. In many places there be Pyramids set up, which are said long since to be brought out of Egypt: of these [348] you shall see at *Santa Maria Maggiore,* Saint Peter's, and other places. There is moreover no house of any worth, that is not replenished with infinite numbers of ancient Statues; so that a man might think, in respect of the number, that in ancient time the inhabitants were employed about nothing else.

14   A domed turret-like erection on the roof of the hall with lateral openings for escaping smoke or entering light.
15   With careful art, skilfully, elaborately, exquisitely, cunningly.

Courts, Galleries, every room is adorned with them, and in many rooms heaped one upon another, there be so many. And yet, for all this multitude, it is a strange thing to see at what inestimable prices they hold every one of them; nay, it is almost an impossibility, by any means, or for any money to get one of them away, they hold them in so great estimation. Nevertheless, every day amongst their Vineyards, and [349] in the ruins of old Rome, they find more, which, in whose ground soever they be found, at a certain price, do now belong to the Popes, who distribute them in their own Palaces, to their favorites or kinsmen, and sometimes as presents to Princes. And this is the cause that the houses of such as have been Nephews or favorites of the Popes, be best furnished with these ornaments.

If a man should make an exact relation of the *Anticaglie*[16] in this kind, he must have seven years time to view, and two men's lives to write them. But for a taste and so away, at the Pope's Palace at Saint Peter's, the Statues of Commodus and Antoninus, the Statue of Laocoön, which is written of by Virgil in the [350] second book of his *Aeneid,* and they say that his very seeing of that Statue, was the cause of those verses: the Statue of Apollo: and in the midst of this place the thigh of a man done in Marble, which the best workmen have judged admirable in the true proportions; and they say that Michelangelo stood two days by it in contemplation, and the artifice was so excellent, and beyond his apprehension, that he had like to have gone mad with the consideration of it. In this place there be many more Antiquities, the great Pine Apple[17] of brass, wherein were found Adrian's ashes. At the Pope's other Palace upon *Mons Quirinalis,* before the Gate, there be two other Statues done in full proportion, of Alexander, taming Bucephalus, [351] made by those two famous men Phydias and Praxiteles, one in emulation of the other. And from these two Statues being set here, this place is called *Monte Cavalli.* In the Garden of Cardinal Borghese without *Porta Pinciana,* there is a Tomb which is said to be Alexander's. In the Palace of Cardinal Farnese, amongst an infinite number of other Antiquities, there

16 Antiquities (Italian).
17 The shape Hobbes suggests here was most likely that of a pine cone, since the pineapple was not much known in early seventeenth-century England.

be the Statues of the twelve first Emperors, two Tables of the Grecians' Laws, which the Romans brought from thence, one of the gods which is said to have given answers in the Pantheon, a Statue of the two sons of a King of Thebes, after the death of their father, tying his Concubine to a Bull, in revenge of those wrongs she had done their mother, (this [352] Story is said to be related by Propertius and Pliny) brought to this City by the ancient Romans out of Rhodes, found in the time of Paulus, III. of the Farnesian family, and by him left as a relic to this house. Here are besides the ancient Statues of the Horatii and Curiatii, and such another of Nero's Mother as I have mentioned to be in the Capitol, but better expressed. In one of the Palaces of Cardinal Borghese, which in former times has been the Kings' of England, and given by Henry VIII to Cardinal Campeio,[18] at his being here; now enriched by the best hands of Painters, and the most ancient Statues; you shall see amongst the rest a Gladiator (or Fencer) admirably described in Marble, and a Statue of Seneca in brass, bleeding in [353] his bath to death, with whom this part also of the Roman Antiquities shall die.

Now from these ancient ruins of Temples, Trophies, Statues, Arches, Columns, Pyramids, and the rest, there would be required in a curious pen a particular observation, but I will only prescribe unto myself some general notes. How venerable Antiquities both be and have been in all men's esteem, is so generally known and received, as I will not enter into a Laudatory thereof, further than to show the singular use and profit that may be gathered from the knowledge of them.

First, they much illustrate Story,[19] and in some cases illuminate the understanding of the Reader, and serve as a confirmation of that he [354] has read. When actions of note be registered, the bare after-reading of then., without seeing the place whence they proceeded, is by many men not so constantly retained in memory. For every man knows, that if in reading an History (only by a Map) the place be observed as well as the action, one's judgment is better strengthened, and consequently much more when a man sees that which others

18 Hobbes refers to Cardinal Lorenzo Campeggio (1474–1539).
19 History.

have but by description. They that have read of Antoninus, Trajan, and Vespasian, and find their acts which they have read engraven in Arches, Pillars, and the like, it is hard to express what credit they give to the History, and satisfaction to the Reader. And if in this respect, any place in the world deserve seeing, [355] none can sooner claim it than Rome.

Secondly, the ancient Statues of the Romans, do strangely immortalize their fame; and it is certain that the men of those times were infinitely ambitious, to have their memories in this kind, recorded; and such was the benignity of that people, that they willingly yielded to honor their acts, by public expression, and in a kind, to Deify the persons of their worthiest men, which industry of theirs may be gathered by the numbers of Statues of Cicero, Seneca, Brutus, Cassius, the Horatii, and Curiatii, Cato, and many more, whose virtue, more than their greatness, made them famous. Otherwise if I had only seen the Statues of the most powerful men, and ancient Emperors, I [356] should have thought there had been in those times as great Timeservers, as there be now, where power and authority is more esteemed of than virtue or valor. Yet I think, if ever men of any place, in any time desired to have their names and actions to continue to Posterity, not knowing any farther immortality, these were they, and this one consideration produced better effects of virtue and valor, than Religion, and all other respects[20] do in our days. Certainly, therefore, if they had been as well instructed in Divine, as Moral precepts, no man of any age had ever exceeded them.

Thirdly, the multitude and riches of these Statues, and other Antiquities, do wonderfully argue the magnificence of those times, wherein [357] they have exceeded all that went before, or followed after them; and yet this sumptuousness nothing diverted their minds from a generous and active life, but rather instigated them; which now we most commonly find contrary. For greatness and goodness do not always agree together.

Fourthly, the Architecture of many ancient Temples, and

20 A consideration; a fact or motive which assists in, or leads to, the formation of a decision; an end or aim—as commonly used in the seventeenth century.

Statues, is so singular and rare, that they that ever since have been esteemed the best, dared never assume, or undertake, to equalize[21] them in that kind of singularity,[22] especially of the Statues, which are so done, that never any could come near the original for exquisiteness in taking the Copy: so that a man cannot but gather, that in this [358] place, and those times, there were conjoined all singularities together, best workmen, best wits, best Soldiers, and so in every kind Superlative.

But it may be there are some, who will draw ill conclusions from these Antiquities, either tending to Atheism, or Superstition. For Atheism thus: If men desire to immortalize their memories in this kind after their death, it may seem the only happiness (being dead) they can expect, is by this means to continue their fame for those acts which living they performed, and have thought of no other immortality than this sort of continuing their memory. And this may seem to be the end of such as in these modern times make Monuments, or have left order for some [359] to be erected after their death in their memory.

To this I will not deny, but that these peradventure might be the farthest ends the Romans aimed at. But amongst us the erection of them is free from the corruption. For first, where the end is out of a religious care to constitute some place for our bodies to remain in, till the day of the general account, I cannot see what more blame can be ascribed to any, for adorning these, than their habitation while they live. And besides, in respect that these be usually set in public places, which is an ornament to them, they are therefore the more allowable. Again, in respect of the benefit and use to such as live, they be not unnecessary; for if they be of such, whose virtues [360] have deserved perpetuity in our memory, they breed a kind of emulation to imitate; if otherwise, their lives have deserved contempt, it is an expression of God's justice, who has suffered such men, who have lived scandalously all their lives, so far to

21 To match or rival.
22 Distinction due to, or involving, some superior quality; special excellence or goodness. The *OED* uses an excerpt from this sentence in the *Horae* as an example of this obsolete usage.

be blinded, that they perpetuate their shame to posterity, and by such men's Monuments, those who have heard of their vices, seek to avoid them.

Again, there be others, who to set a gloss upon their Atheistical opinions, argue thus. If the Romans of that time, who were ever reputed men of most acute judgment, and reverenced for their gravity and understanding, thought their chiefest happiness after death to consist in those outward respects, why should it be thought in this declining [361] age of the world, where men for learning and height of wit come short of those which preceded, that we should find new ways of immortality, which the elder world never dreamed of, and charge those who have ever been so much esteemed for their wisdom, with so gross an ignorance? To this it may be answered: First, that these Romans had some sense of the immortality of the soul, but in what manner, and way, being only guided by natural reason and learning, they were utterly ignorant. "For there is none but the fool that has said in his heart, that there is no God."[23] Again, it is not all the learning or wit of man, can find out the mystery of true religion, without God's blessing and holy Spirit to assist them. But to such as these, who are only [362] learned in natural sciences, and had no inspiration from above: how can they but (as the Apostle says) count the manifestations of Religion foolishness? So that this argument must be no derogation to the truth of Religion, for that learned men heretofore understood it not.

For the other error that may be drawn from these Antiquities, inclining to Superstition, which may be defined to be a Religion exercised in false worship. In those times, these durable Monuments tended that way: for either men were so ambitious to expect Deification, or people so foolish to give it them, ascribing miraculous operation to their dead Images. Which error needs no confutation: for all men see the Arrogance [363] of them that desired, and simplicity of such as gave belief to these vain imaginations. And yet I cannot but admire at the strange blindness of such, who in this clear Sunshine of Christianity, have such a mist before their eyes (imaginary not

23   Cf. Ps. 14:1 or 53:1.

real) that they will still turn the image of the incorruptible God, into the likeness of a corruptible man, which in any natural understanding, seems foolish, in a religious, profane. I dare walk no farther in this Labyrinth, for fear of growing too infinite,[24] only this, it is the wonder of the world, that men should be so far carried away with this Idiotism,[25] which is both against Reason and Religion.

Now in the next place after profane, the religious Antiquities of [364] this place deserves consideration in which, I profess a greater brevity, than in that which is past. Of the seven Churches, to which men go upon extraordinary devotion, the first is Saint Peter's, now in re-edifying,[26] of a great length, with an answerable breadth. You ascend unto it by many stairs, where, at the first view, is presented the most goodly *Facciata*, or forefront of the world, supported with many great pillars of Marble. This Church is very high, and upon the top of the *Cupola*, or circumference, is a Ball of brass, which to them below seems no bigger than an ordinary Bowl, yet is of that capacity, that it will receive at least forty persons. The inside of this Rotunda within the Church is most curiously painted with the [365] acts of Christ and his Apostles. The finishing of the high Altar is undertaken by the King of Spain. The lower part of this round is adorned with Mosaic work, and the Altar compassed about with those pillars of Marble which are said to have been in Solomon's Temple, they being curiously carved and fashioned in the form of wreaths. On the left hand in a Chapel where the Canons sing their Office is the Statue of our Lady, and Christ in her arms, cut in Marble by the most famous Painter and Statuist[27] in the World, Michelangelo. Within a vault of this Church be the bodies of Saint Peter and Saint Paul. Here also be seven Chapels resembling the seven Churches which be usually visited. Adjoining to this Church is

24   Occupying an indefinitely long time; immensely long, very tedious. This is the example used in the *OED*.
25   Extreme folly. This sentence is the example used in the *OED*. It can also mean "void of intellect or reason."
26   Rebuilding.
27   Sculptor. This sentence is the *OED* example.

[366] the Pope's Palace of Saint Peter's, and from thence a *Curridore*,[28] or private way, to his Castle of Saint Angelo. In this Palace the Consistories usually assemble, and here is the Conclave where the Popes be elected. There is also a private Chapel of the Popes where the high Altar is set out by Michelangelo's curious description of the day of Judgment. Besides, in this Palace is the Vatican, or famous Library of the Popes, which consists only of Manuscripts, but of great antiquity, as well profane, as divine. Besides, all correspondences, and matters of State, that are and have been betwixt the Pope and other Princes be here registered. This Palace has been sundry times enlarged by divers Popes.

[367] The second of the seven Churches is *Santa Maria Maggiore*, seated upon one of the Seven Hills, called *Mons Esquilinus;* upon which goes this Story, that in the time of the Primitive Church, there was a vision appeared to a man and his Wife, that very night the same also appearing to the then Bishop of Rome, that presently in that place where that good man and his Wife lay, there should be a Church built and dedicated to our Lady: and this they say is that Church which was erected for that dream. This Church is famous for these relics. The bodies of Saint Matthew, and Saint Jerome, which lie here buried, The Cope[29] of Saint Thomas Becket, which he wore at his death, and sprinkled with part [368] of the blood which he then lost. And the picture of our Lady drawn, as they say, by Saint Luke. But that which makes this Church now so remarkable, is the two Splendid Chapels, the one built by Sixtus Quintus, where he lies buried, and the other over against it (but more beautiful) by this Pope Paolo V where he is to be buried. In that of Sixtus Quintus, there be carved all his Acts, during his Papacy, but especially the expedition of Ferrara, and in the other, besides his own actions, and Statue, the whole Chapel is most richly and curiously painted, the high Altar standing upon pillars of brass, inlaid with Agate, and besides,

---

28 *Curridore* (from the Latin *currere*, to run) is an older, Latinate form of *corridore;* in this context it corresponds to the modern Italian *corridoio* and is best translated as "corridor" or "passageway."

29 Cape, in this case a specific type of ecclesiastical vestment.

in many places adorned with stones of inestimable price. To relate particularly, the magnificence [369] of both these, would ask a longer Narration than I purpose.

The third of these Churches is Saint Paul's, without the town, about a mile and a half in *Via Ostia:* here is underneath, the grottos or Caves, wherein, as in others about Rome, the Christians in time of persecution were wont to conceal themselves, and make their private conventions.

The fourth in this way also, and without the town, is consecrated to the memory of Saints Sebastian and Fabian. In one of the Altars here made of Marble, and about a foot thick, you shall see a little hole, in compass about the bigness of a twenty shillings piece. Of which there goes this Tale, that a Priest in the celebration of Mass, and at the time of the consecration, had [370] an imagination of the impossibility, how upon the saying of the words used in the consecration, the host should be converted really into the body of Christ: whereupon the host suddenly and miraculously vanished out of his hand, and made this way specified, proportionable to that bigness.

The fifth without *Porta Esquilina,* is that of Saint Lawrence, where his body is interred. This Church was built by Constantine the Great, and those instruments wherewith they were wont to sacrifice Christians, be here to be seen, and more particularly, the Gridiron whereupon it is said Saint Lawrence was broiled.

The sixth is *Santa Croce,* one of the principallest Churches of devotion, [371] built by Helena, mother to Constantine. The ground upon which this Church is built is of the holy earth brought by her from Jerusalem. Amongst other Relics, there is a part of the Cross, from whence it took the name, and one of the thorns of that Crown, which was in derision set upon our Savior's head.

Now the last of these is that of Saint John the Lateran, where the Lateran Council was held. The heads of Saint Peter, and Saint Paul be here retained for Relics. The pillars that support the Altar in this Church, are said to be brought from Jerusalem to Rome by Vespasian. Here is the Font where Constantine was baptized by Pope Silvester. Besides, the pillars are thought to have been taken [372] out of Pilate's house, and that upon one of them stood that Cock which by his twice crow-

ing gave Peter warning of his sin. Here in the *Sanctum Sancto-
rum,* (where women cannot enter) is also conserved the Ark of
the old Testament, Aaron's Rod, The Sudatorium, which is a
Napkin, with which in the way to the Cross Christ wiping his
face, there remained in it his picture; the Table upon which
Christ celebrated his last Supper, and one little Glass of his
Blood. At the entrance of this Church be those Stairs, brought
from Jerusalem, by which Christ ascended when he entered
Pilate's house, some twenty in number, whereupon daily many
people go up, upon their knees for devotion, upon every one
saying a *Pater noster,* and an *Ave* [373] *Maria,* and then kissing
it. Some also whip themselves as they go up. And this Church
was also built by Constantine the Great, at the instance of
Pope Sylvester.

To go more particularly in the narration of the holy Relics,
and Monuments of Rome, after the description of the seven
Churches, they are so infinite, that I should be too prolix. This
may serve as a view to the rest, only I will remember one
strange tale in the Church of *San Pietro ad vincula:* Saint Peter
coming to Rome, was cast in Prison, and bound with a chain,
which after his death was kept as an holy Relic: sometime after
this, the chain wherewith he was bound in his imprisonment
at Jerusalem, being by Christians brought to Rome, and into
the [374] place where this other was kept, they, as it may seem,
for joy, being a good distance asunder, leaped together and
joined themselves, and still remain so: so was this Church
builded in remembrance of that miracle, and herewith I will
end this part of my Discourse. Now for my other observations,
that I gather from these holy Antiquities:

First, I must profess for myself, that I am not so credulous,
as to tie my belief to these miraculous reports; nay, I am so far
from it, that I esteem most of them rather feigned than true;
yet such is the Artifice of these popish traders, that they are
fain[30] to sell their commodities by this false light, and to set a
gloss upon their Religion, by these and such like Illusions.

So that here in the next place [375] we are to consider,
how easily men are drawn by circumstances, to think they embrace certainties, by shadows to conclude truth, and by out-

30 Well-pleased, content.

ward show of zeal and Religion, to embrace impiety. Such is
the flexibility of our nature. And by way of digression there
can be nothing more observable, than the variation of minds,
as well as faces. Some have such stony hearts and leaden heads,
that they cannot conceive (beyond themselves, and nature, as
they term it) any supernatural, or powerful government in
their life and actions, nor any heaven, besides their sensuality.
Others so believing, and uncertain, that every tale, or imagination creates in their brains a new Creator, and forces a false
worship. [376] Such are these which I now speak of. A false
miracle prevails farther than the written verity, a Monastical,
and severe seeming habit more persuades, than sincerity in life
and manners; the representation of an image strikes deeper
into their affections, than that way whereby God has made
himself manifest in the Scriptures. So that they are carried
away with every wind; so great is their corruption, so stupid[31]
their senses, so monstrous their ignorance.

By this you may see, it is no difficult matter to persuade
these men's consciences to one's own fancy, and to serve one's
own turn. Alas, an outward show of devotion, and a few good
words carries them into admiration, and to imagine that God
is better pleased [377] with ceremony, than truth, with form
than substance. This trade has been so long, and this deceit so
customary, that many, though otherwise of strong capacities,
are blinded with the same ignorance as it were by prescription:
but if they would but give themselves leave to review the
grounds, upon which they retain these opinions, and search
to the original from whence they sprung, they would quickly
discover the deceit. But if men will believe impossibilities, and
for no other reason, but because other men do so, and their
Fathers did so before them; I can think no otherwise of such
than as of blind men, who are to follow their leaders, and may
be sometimes drawn into the ditch.[32] A man might spin out a
long Discourse of such a [378] subject: but thus much shall
serve for this observation upon the Religious antiquities, and
Relics of Rome.

Now in order, but very briefly, as before, Antiquities pro-

31 Deadened or dull, as in a stupor.
32 The allusion is to Matthew 15:14.

fane, and then Religious were considered; so now the present buildings, and pleasures, and next the more modern houses of Religion be to be discoursed of.

For the first, I will only for a taste, name some few places, by which you may guess the rest. There be in this town multiplicity of Palaces, which for Architecture, and curiosity, may compare with any City of the world, of which, I will but nominate two. The first is a house newly built by this Pope, at the foot of *Monte Quirinale*, or *Cavalli*, given to his [379] brother's son the Prince of Sulmo (a Principality in the Kingdom of Naples) built round, and standing upon Pillars of Marble, divided into three heights, separated by Terraces, and every one standing alike upon Pillars. The Court, Terraces, and particular Chambers adorned with antique Statues, many of the rooms being most curiously painted both upon the top and sides, and equal rooms in all three heights, both for pleasure and use.

The second is a Palace beyond *Porta Pinciana*, built by Cardinal Borghese, this Pope's Sister's son, a house full of pleasure, and spacious, where about the middle, from room to room, the doors being open, you may see in a direct line, the whole length of the house, as [380] it were a prospective,[33] a kind of curiosity very much followed in the best buildings of Italy.

Now for houses of pleasure, gardens, waterworks and the like; there is that Garden-house (as I may term it) of Borghese, near *Monte Quirinale*, built in that place where Propertius the Poet lived. This is very pleasant, not many rooms, but three or four Gardens, enriched with divers Statues, and Fountains. Then there is that of the Belvedere by Saint Peter's, which is the Pope's, and another garden rare for Fruits adjoining to it. That Garden of Cardinal Bandino, by the Noviceship of the Jesuits, towards *Santa Maria Maggiore*, has Statues and Fountains in it, and is all vaulted, the better to take the fresh air in the heat of Summer. [381] Then the Garden joining to the Pope's Palace at *Monte Cavallo*, is very splendid: but amongst those, and all the other Gardens of Rome, which be most remarkable, those of Montalto, Maffei, and Lanfranc, be the

33   A view or a place for viewing.

three rarest for pleasure, beauty, store of banqueting houses, Fountains, and other delicacies, that can add ornament to such places: and thus much of this division.

From hence I observe that as man's life ought to be sustained with those necessities which most uphold it; so there may be an addition of lawful delights, and pleasures, to comfort and refresh it. For there is no man, or mind, so retired, but requires some delight, and pleasure: otherwise the sharpness of our apprehension would be [382] tired, and the progress of our life, solitary; it being an impossibility, and Solecism in nature,[34] for a man continually to travel[35] without intermixture of recreation, because we be so subject, as well in body, as in mind, to variation.

And in this kind I know few recreatives[36] that possess us more, than the humor of building, in respect they both satisfy our own present invention, and serve to our posterity, as perpetual remembrances, and memorials of their progenitors, adding present content to ourselves, perpetuating reputation in the world, remaining as living Monuments of our magnificence, and beneficent expressions of our greatness.

And although munificence in this kind, be by many esteemed [383] superfluous, I rather hold it convenient, so it be of our abundance, and diminish nothing of the competency of our estates. If it should do so, it were too great an argument of our folly, to propose unnecessary charges. Otherwise these respects might make it allowable.

First, this Art of Architecture is honorable in all men's esteem, and profitable to ourselves. Next, it keeps us busied in thought, and action, and so diverts us from delights more dangerous. Then upon occasion it enables us in the use of fortification. Fourthly, it gives a kind of extraordinary delight to ourselves, when we see those things, which before we had but formed in conceit, made visible. Next, it is an addition [384] of repute to the City where we live. And lastly, it makes a man's fame to spread both at home, and abroad.

34 Violation of nature.
35 In the seventeenth century this could mean labor (travail).
36 Amusement or diversion that refreshes. This sentence is used in the *OED* as the example.

But to descend more particularly to the pleasures of this place, the delicacy of Gardens be of inestimable consideration, where a man's mind may receive such content, and his eye such diversity of objects, as in nothing more. If a place of delight and pleasure content our minds, it may here be satisfied with the beauty of walks, sweetness and diversity of Flowers, melody of Birds, and the like. If sometimes a man be inclined to melancholy, the privacy and solitude of this place, the murmuring of the waters, fills us with a strange kind of satisfaction. If one would contemplate the wonders of nature, [385] here he may find all things necessary, and pleasurable; healthful, or hurtful for man. If we be inclined to any serious study, or meditation, here is the place where our thoughts cannot be perturbed, nor diverted, nor our senses unsharpened, because they continually meet with such variation. If you meditate, sit by the fountain, or walk in the most remote and obscure places. When you would read, or write, then are there Arbors and Banqueting houses to repose in. And to conclude, if at any time a man would desire to give himself, and some few of his friends, the height of civil entertainment, no place can be more apt than this, especially in the heat of Summer, in a Country so subject to the violence of it as Rome is.

[386] If a man were [more] Poetical, than this discourse, he could not find a better field to exercise his wit. The Houses of these places be adorned with many rarities, but especially painting, the praise and excellency whereof is sufficiently known; so that I will forbear the repetition: and thus I conclude this consideration.

In the next place, the present Colleges, Churches, and religious Houses come in turn, in which of late years, those of the Jesuits be of principal reputation, where in their chief Church lies buried their founder Ignatius, and his Tomb is there to be seen. There be besides divers Churches appropriate to several nations, as that of Saint Apolinarius, to the Germans, Saint James, to the Spaniards, Saint [387] Stanislaus, to the Polacks, a Church dedicated to the holy Trinity, built by Louis the eleventh King of France, to the French, and another dedicated to the holy Trinity, for the English.

There is their College, and in the Church be the Tombs of Cardinal Allen, and Parsons; upon the walls whereof be set forth in painting, the Martyrdoms (as they call it) of such as suffered persecution, and death, for their Religion in England. And in this, now amongst the rest are Campion, and Garnet, and the Hangman, and Tyborne, as perfectly described as if they were better acquainted with the place, and person. Here is also a Library consisting most of Controversies. To the maintenance of this Church, and College, there be [388] some lands appointed, besides other pensions that they receive from the Pope, and King of Spain. The persons here be all English and were governed by a Rector of the Jesuits' order, called Father Owen, lately dead. They are all Priests, and young Youths, sent thither out of England, to be brought up in Philosophy, and Divinity, in number about 120, all going in the habit of Scholars, and no sooner come thither, but they take upon them false and suppositious names, as the Rector himself told me.

This town is full of Monasteries, and Religious houses, many public Schools, where Divinity and Philosophy are read in Lectures, and many public Libraries. Besides, there be sundry Hospitals for strangers, [389] maimed, poor, sick, and mad folks. The number of the Churches be about 140. And so I will leave this part.

Now for my observation, it is this, to show the Policy that they use for confirmation, and establishing of their Religion, and consists, first, in an outward show of devotion, with strange expressions of humility, set forth in the poor and austere life of many orders, in their sundry acts of penitence, in their daily visitation of their Churches, in their outward actions of grief, and repentance at the celebration of Mass. Wherein is inserted all possible inventions, to catch men's affections, and to ravish their understanding: as first, the gloriousness of their Altars, infinite numbers of images, priestly ornaments, [390] and the divers actions they use in that service; besides the most excellent and exquisite Music of the world, that surprises our ears. So that whatsoever can be imagined, to express either Solemnity, or Devotion, is by them used.

Their next way, is in their acts of Charity, wherein they exceed, and imagine this a great argument to make the world believe the truth, and certainty of their Religion.

The third is, their boasting of miracles, with which they

make such a noise, and would have them infallible arguments, to uphold their faith: but when a man sees the ridiculousness, and finds proved the falsity of them, they are of great force to persuade the contrary. For example, if a man going down a pair of stairs, by chance [391] his foot should slip, he would presently make a miracle of it, and say, that in that instant he called upon Saint Francis, or San Carlo, or some other Saint, by whose prayers he was relieved, that otherwise he had maimed himself, or lost his life. Or if in riding in a Coach, it by chance be overthrown, he presently attributes to some Saint whom he then invoked, the liberation of him from an imminent danger: and with the expressions of these miracles, all the Churches be hung full.

But for others that be more strange, it is certain, and has been proved, that many of them are false, and broached only to delude the people, which may give a great suspicion to the rest. But more, it is the Jesuits' doctrine, and they labor to prove it lawful, to forge a miracle [392] for the furtherance of their Religion. By which Position, if any thing happen, which may seem a wonder, as in the recovery of some desperate sickness, wound, or the like, in the attribution of it to some particular Saint, or extraordinary operation by their means, they diminish the power and glory of God. And if any sign should happen to confirm it, of which they will nominate thousands, as the bleeding of a Crucifix, the speaking of an Image, etc. It may as well show the now delusive power of the Devil, still blinding the eyes of the world in this kind, as he has formerly done by Oracles.

Now the last policy is, in the course of their teaching, and disciplining, which I will only exemplify [393] by the practice of our English there. First, there shall no scandal pass, that they will not be sure to lay upon our Religion.[37] And this at the first they beat and insinuate into the ears of their Novices. Next, they use all possible Art to magnify their own: in the meantime, barring the reading of any defense of our parts, and put them to study such books as be written against us; so that they will conclude a Judgment, before both parts be heard. But when they have them more strongly grounded, and

---

37 Here Hobbes refers to the Church of England.

they be sure that their opinion is prejudicated,[38] they will suffer them then to read some of our books (but by the way, this liberty is seldom given to Italians) and then for ourselves, [394] that be so strongly instructed of one side, and strangely opinionated of the other, he is a rare man, and receives from God a great blessing, that ever finds the true difference. And thus being woven in their nets, they be in a manner destitute of all possibility of recovery. And so much for this.

Now next in order it follows, that something be said of the present strength of this place, and of what force it is against foreign, or domestic enemies. And in my opinion it is of no great power. For examples have showed, that it has suffered divers surprises; so that of necessity it must be of less ability now to withstand than before. For place of strength, it has only the Castle of Saint Angelo, and that also very weak, to withstand any [395] strong assault. But the truth is, there be so many Princes in league with this See,[39] and tied in so divers obligations unto it, that it is free from danger, without the Turk should make a war;[40] and then there is so strong opposition like to be made by the Princes of Italy, and other foreigners, that it will be hard to prevail against it, if the Emperor, Italy itself, the King of France and Spain, should not cast off their yoke and subjection: if so, then it were impossible for the Bishop of Rome by his own strength, to oppose or subsist.

Now for the government of this place, it is wholly subject to the Pope, which he holds as a temporal prince, but solely guided by spiritual Ministers; all causes of judgment in matters divine are [396] brought hither, as to the last Court of Appeal for final sentences.

For the Pope's Revenue: that which he receives from his own principalities, is the least part; the rest consists in the Fair[41] of Indulgences, liberation from Purgatory, conferring of Church-livings,[42] sale of Offices, Pensions from other Princes,

---

38 Judged, settled, or decided beforehand.
39 Spelled "Sea" in the original, this refers to a place or seat, and particularly the building, city, or territory where the official residence or throne of a bishop is located, in this case the pope, the bishop of Rome.
40 Meaning, "*unless* the Turk should make a war . . ."
41 Market or sale.
42 Livings (income) or benefices in an established church.

and the like. The treasure is never great, in respect of the changes of their Governors, who for the most part have employed all the Revenue of the Church to their own private families, and friends. If upon occasion they be forced to make any great, and sudden supply, they make bold with the treasures and ornaments of Churches, which be in Italy of very great value.

[397] Now to the person of this Pope: he is descended of no great family, an Italian born, and exercised the former part of his life, before his Papacy, in the office of a Judge. He was made Cardinal by Clement the eighth, and Pope by the difference of the two great factions, in that conclave of Montalto, and Aldobrandino; both striving to make one of their own creatures, yet finding the other opposition too strong, were in the end forced to make a neutral. And so by this fortune it lighted upon this man. His Court is not great (some small guard of Switzers excepted) but he rather lives a kind of retired life; the chiefest of his actions tending to the advancement of his Kindred. He is most governed by his Nephew the Cardinal [398] Borghese, but for matter of greatness in correspondence with the greatest Princes, he is behind none, having Ambassadors from, and sending to them, more than any other temporal Prince whatsoever. And when he shows himself, it is in as great majesty, and with more ceremony than is used to any other Prince, which for exemplification shall be showed in the custom that is used of kissing his feet, and the manner of his carrying in a chair when he goes publicly.

For the first, upon his Pantofle[43] there is a cross, which people in show of their reverence and devotion, kiss at the time of his giving audience to Ambassadors, or some other public assembly: and this is to show the people's reverence to [399] his person, and to set forth his own dignity. And the sign of the Cross upon it, is to declare that in that action, the people's devotion to our Savior, as well as honor to him, might be expressed, and in a kind, for acknowledgement, that Religion is under his government, and subjection. For his being carried in a chair upon men's shoulders, they urge this to be used as an argument of his sanctity, and holiness, to stir up

43 Slipper.

reverence in the beholders, and devotion in their hearts, and that as all outward respects be used to honor the Princes of the world, so there ought to be much more to the Pope, being head of the Church. In this kind he is usually carried, when he goes to Church or Consistory.

[400] Now to end this part with the Cardinals: it is strange to see their pride, every one esteeming himself of equal rank with any Prince, and are served with a kind of extraordinary pomp, using in their rooms of audience, clothes of estate, as Princes do, and when they go to Consistory, you shall have one of them attended by their friends and followers with 20 or 30 Coaches, and at least 200 or 300 *Staffieri* or footmen. Some in this kind exceed others, but the principal be Montalto, that was Sixtus Quintus, and Aldobrandino, that was Clement the eighth, and Borghese, that is this Pope's favorite. Some others live more retired, of which rank Bellarmine is chiefly noted. Most of them be in faction Spanish, and all receiving [401] bribes and pensions from him. Their creation comes either from the Pope's particular favor, or some great Prince's intercession; younger brothers of great families, and all in a manner by the way of the present favorite, who enriches himself, and makes his faction great, by the distribution of these honors. I only saw them once assembled together, and that was in the Pope's private Chapel, at Saint Peter's, upon All Saints' even,[44] when the Pope sang Vespers or Evensong: there were in number of them about some 30. I think, all that were then in Rome.

Where I observed 3 things: first, their places, all fitting round about the Chapel; secondly, their habits, of Scarlet; thirdly, their reverence to the Pope, in the time that the [402] Anthem was sung, every one in his rank, one after another, rising out of their seats, and going to his chair, which is by the Altar: where they adore him in this kind, by bending their bodies, kneeling, and kissing his garments.

Amongst these Cardinals I principally observed two: one for his learning, and that was Bellarmine, a little lean old man; the other was Cardinal Tosco, and he, at the Conclave when this Pope was chosen, was so near being chosen, that many yet

44 Eve.

think the election went on his side. For of 60 he had 45 voices.
But when he was set in his Chair, and they coming to adore
him, Baronius came in and said, "Will you choose him head of
the Church, that cannot speak a sentence without that scurri-
lous byword[45] of the [403] Lombards (*Cazzo*)?[46] What a shame
will this be in our election?" And upon this divers of his voices
fell from him, and he lost the Popedom.

Now for that I gather from this place, which shall be very
short, it is this; That the sumptuousness of the Pope, and the
pride of his government, is one token of the falsity of their
doctrine; seeing they which pretend to have rule over, and to
give direction unto others, are tainted with this leprosy. For it
is never seen that the body is sound, when the head is corrupt,
and it is impossible for any to guide another, that stumbles in
his own way, or to be a director to others, that stands in his
own light.

More particularly, for these Prelates: it is quite contrary to
the ordinance [404] of God, and different from the example
of Christ, and his Apostles, to challenge temporal jurisdiction
or superiority, when their charge is only to instruct. And they
who should be examples for others to imitate, in life and conversation, and in that kind to teach as well by example as precept, what instruction can we gather from them, but ambitious
thoughts, and unsatisfied desires after the wealth and glory of
this world?

Again, their excess in this kind is unnecessary; for what
can be pretended for these Popes and other Ecclesiastical persons, that they should so violently desire honor, and superfluity
in wealth? Are they not, by their own rules, in a manner, separated from the world, and barred from any [405] hope of successors in their own posterity? Therefore one should imagine
these so immoderate desires, impertinent. And it could be no
diminution either to the glory or progress of Religion; for the
very function itself is honorable and reverenced; and moderate attributions both of dignity and living ought to be ascribed
them. But why all should be included within this center, and

45 Epithet of scorn.
46 This Italian expletive was a colloquial term for the penis.

wholly referred to the person of the Pope, I neither see for it Reason, nor Religion.

But lastly, this extremity of their pride is advantageous against them, and gives dangerous examples even amongst themselves. When the People be taught moderation and sobriety, and see excess and liberty in their teachers, none is [406] so blind but must see their deceit. When they are instructed in acts of charity, and persuaded to impoverish themselves to enrich a Priest, who can shadow[47] their cozenage?[48] When they pronounce Indulgences, and we pay for them; what man can think the Pope has so much interest in God, as to make him pardon us, for his profit? When they profess sanctity and strictness of life; who will believe him, when, after he has gotten to be a Bishop or Cardinal, he is found to be as proud, seditious and covetous as the rest? When the Pope professes poverty, and as they say in his procession, when he is elected, being carried publicly to show himself to the world, hurls brass amongst the people, and uses these words of Saint Peter, "Gold and silver [407] have I none, but that which I have, I give unto thee,"[49] what man perceives not their abusing of the Scripture, and mocking of the people? When the Pope, to show his humility upon the Maundy Thursday, washes the feet of the poor, and in the meantime is attended with Cardinals, and Ambassadors, some giving him water, some the towel, others holding his train, himself carried into, and out of the room, as if he were too good to tread on the earth; what man can be so stupid that discerns not his pride? Thus you may see what contrariety there is betwixt their profession and practice. And so I will leave this observation.

And now to draw to a conclusion: after this description I do not [408] think it unnecessary to say something of the safety and danger for an English man to travel thither. And I am the rather induced unto it, because I have heard from many that have been there, such strange tales, and such wonders of their escape, as if they meant to scare us with Rome, as children be here with Hobgoblins.

47 Conceal or obscure.
48 Deception or fraud.
49 Acts 3:6.

It is true, that for some persons there can be no place in the world so dangerous for them to come in, as this; and they are such, as have been noted either to be extreme persecutors of them, violently addicted[50] against them, or such as have opposed them by public disputation, or writing, in matter of Controversy; for these, it is certain, if they be found, they shall be either brought into the Inquisition, or [409] forced to be reconciled to their Church. And yet I do not think it impossible for any of this sort to make a Voyage thither, and never be surprised; but then they must neither publish their purpose nor time; for the English there, have eyes and ears in all places, and such a man is no sooner gone, or purposes to go out of England, but they hear of it, and he can live in no place of Italy, but they have intelligence of him. Therefore the safest course for such a one, is to pass that, before he settle in any other place, and in the meantime neither to make himself, nor intention known to anybody living, for then there may be a possibility of discovery. And besides it is necessary, that he have some other Language besides his [410] own, that he may pass for that Countryman: and amongst some of them he should troop himself,[51] and be careful also, that with them he never show any disaffection to the Religion; for then they may grow jealous, and discover him. Besides, I would not have him stay there too long, nor converse with any of his own Nation.

There be some others also that may not come hither safely; and they are of this sort, who though themselves have in no action given them cause of offense, yet some of their name or Kindred, either were or be professed enemies against them. Others also are endangered here, if they have any [411] particular enemy, that is great in, or has interest with any of the College (for no Englishman is put into the Inquisition, unless he give some public offense but by their means) then peradventure he may be brought into trouble, only upon revenge and malice.

But for others, and specially men of Quality, their coming hither may be with as much freedom, as to any other part of Italy. I myself have, and have met with divers that do find it so,

---

50 Inclined.
51 To associate or consort with a number of others, to go in company. This is the example used in the *OED*.

and therefore, I believe it, whatsoever other men say to the contrary, to grace, or make wonderful their own Travels.

Now after the person, those actions which may bring a man into danger, ought to be avoided. If a [412] man, in his going thither, or being there, converse with Italians, and disclose, or dispute his Religion, he is sure, unless he fly, to be complained on, and brought within the Inquisition. For they hold it an act of merit, to discover an Heretic (as they term us) thinking that by this means we may be drawn from our Religion, and the honor of our conversion (as they call it) must be attributed to them.

Next, when you are in the Church, or near any Relic, Cross, or Procession in the street; you must give no scandal, nor seem to be singular from the actions of other men: but if you be desirous to avoid their superstition, you must forebear coming into their Churches, at Mass time, or Vespers, and beware of their street encounters.

[413] Thirdly, in the place where you lie, you must be careful to observe their Fasts, and not be curious[52] in desiring, or seeming to desire such fare as those days will not admit.

Besides, it ought to be one of our principal cares, lest in any place where we should reside, before our coming thither, we show ourselves too bitter and violent against our Nation there, especially in their persons; for that may exasperate, if it come to their knowledge.

Fifthly, it is a mere folly in any man that has lived publicly in any town of Italy, before he come thither to hide and conceal himself there, for he cannot live undiscovered: and peradventure this jealousy of ours, and distrust of them, may produce some mischief [414] against us, which otherwise they would never dream of. But some will be so quick, that they will come to Rome, and away before they have half slept. And certainly, such dispositions, I think, they had even as good lived in England, with their Nurses, and would have there got as much experience, I am sure, as much wit.[53]

---

52 Attracting attention.
53 Hobbes opines that travelers to Rome who leave again so soon might just as profitably have remained at home where they could enjoy the care and advice of their nurses and gain as much experience and awareness of the world.

Sixthly, I hold it very dangerous, for a man that is known to be there, to go about to cozen[54] the College, and make them believe he is a Papist, when there is no such matter. For this dissimulation may cause them to force him to express that which he affirms, by some act, that may foil[55] his Religion. And therefore, methinks, it is a strange Arrogance in those people, to go about to deceive them, that know [415] their Religion, and Character, as well as themselves.

Next, in your conversation, show (and so peradventure you may have cause) to express a thankfulness for those courtesies you receive: and though they give you cause to speak something in the defense of your Religion, show no violence, nor reply not too much, by which you shall argue your own temper, and give them less cause to urge you. For heat in disputation, especially where a man comes with disadvantage, shows folly in us, and stirs malice in them.

Now the final caveat is, that by no means you go about to persuade any from thence, though formerly your friend, and near acquaintance. For you must believe, [416] that they who dare let him converse with you, be sure that he will discover[56] whatsoever you say, and there is not any one thing, will sooner breed a mischief against us, than the attempting to divert one from their society.

The last point that a man is to enter into consideration upon, when he travels to Rome, is the time. First, those times of public hostility, as in the Reign of Queen Elizabeth, when the Pope thundered excommunications, and professed himself an open enemy to the State, as he did then, it is dangerous. Next, if the Governor of the English there, were of so violent and malicious a disposition as Parsons[57] was, there were little

54 Deceive.
55 Hobbes's text reads *foyle*, which is an obsolete form for three words—*foal*, *foil*, and *fool*. *Foil*, which is most likely for this spelling, could mean to trample (in mud), defeat, or oppress. But it also meant to foul, defile, or pollute. Especially in reference to mistreatment of women it meant to dishonor or violate. See the earlier usage at page 37, line 21, and note 15.
56 Disclose or reveal.
57 Robert Parsons (sometimes spelled Persons), 1546–1610, an English Jesuit who helped establish seminaries for English Catholics in France and Italy. He was a famous controversialist, due largely to his conspiracies which sought

safety. Thirdly, in the time of the holy week, because then there is an exact [417] view, and every householder is to render an account of those strangers he entertains, that they have confessed, communicated, and the like. Fourthly, if a man should enter into any quarrel, and be apprehended by the Temporal Magistrate, the Inquisition also takes hold of him, and he cannot be delivered till he be reconciled to the Church. And lastly, if a man should fall sick, during the time of his being there, within three days the Physician is to take his oath, that his patient has confessed, and communicated, otherwise he must leave him, and the party be delivered over to the Inquisition before he depart. And thus have I briefly, and sincerely discovered my knowledge of this place.

FINIS.

---

to restore England to the papacy by persuasion or force. His most notorious intrigues included his lobbying of the Spanish monarch for the invasion of England and his work to foment a Scottish Catholic rebellion. He and Cardinal William Allen were close associates who looked out for English interests in Rome in the period preceding Hobbes's visit there. Hobbes describes their tombs in Rome on pages 91–92 [387] above.

A DISCOVRSE OF LAVVES.

He nature of all sorts of *Lawes*, whether they concerne *God*, and *Religion*, and so haue reference to *diuine Lawes*, or whether they concerne *societie*, and *conuersation*, and so be meerely *Humane*, is properly this, to be the straight and perfect rule, by application wherevnto, *right* and *wrong* are discerned, and distingnished one from another:

Mm 2   and

A Discourse of Laws

[505] The nature of all sorts of Laws, whether they concern God, and Religion, and so have reference to divine Laws, or whether they concern society, and conversation,[1] and so be merely Human, is properly this, to be the straight and perfect rule, by application whereunto, right and wrong are discerned, and distinguished one from another: [506] and the knowledge, and practice of them, bring a double benefit, either Public, which is the general good and government of the State; or Private, which consists in the quiet, and peaceable life of everyone in particular. So the true end of all Laws is to ordain, and settle an order, and government amongst us, the Jurisdiction whereof we are rather bound to obey, than dispute; Laws being, as it were, the Princes we ought to serve, the Captains we are to follow, the very rules, by which all the actions of our life be squared[2] and disposed. They are the people's bulwarks, and defenses, to keep them in safety, and peace; that no unjust thing be done against them; that by the Laws men may be made good, and happy; and that the punishment of offenders should [507] appear to proceed from a necessity forced, rather than a will voluntary, and that by the example of punish-

---

1 The *OED* gives two meanings that will not occur immediately to modern readers but seem to fit the context well. The action of living or having one's being *in* a place or *among* persons. 6. Manner of conducting oneself in the world or in society; behavior, mode or course of life.
2 Made fair and equal, harmonized.

ing some, others might be made the better; that by the fear, and terror of them, men's audacities might be repressed, and their innocence, and peace, secured from force and oppression.

If men were not limited within certain rules, such confusion would follow in government, that the differences of Right and wrong, Just and unlawful, could never be distinguished; and that would cause such distraction in the people, and give so great an overthrow to conversation, and commerce amongst men, that all right would be perverted by power, and all honesty swayed by greatness: so that the equal administration of [508] Justice, is the true knot that binds us to unity and peace amongst ourselves, and disperses all such violent and unlawful courses, as otherwise liberty would insinuate, preserving every man in his right, and preventing others, who if they thought their actions might pass with impunity, would not measure their courses, by the rule of Aequum and Justum,[3] but by the square of their own benefit, and affections: and so not being circumscribed within reasonable bounds, their reason becomes invisible; whereas when they find that Justice has a Predominant power, they are deterred from proceeding in those acts, that otherwise their own wills, and inclination would give them leave to effect.

Plato affirms the necessity of [509] Laws to be so great and absolute that men otherwise could not be distinguished from unreasonable creatures: for no man naturally is of so great capacity, as completely to know all the necessities, and accidents[4] which be required for a common good: and then if a man could suppose in any so perfect a knowledge, yet is that man not to be found, that either absolutely could, or would do all that good which he knows: so that in an Utopia of such men as be not, yet the necessity of Laws is absolute.[5] But where men's

3   Hobbes here means "the fair and the just," and uses Latin neuter forms meaning the fair or even and the righteous or equitable, respectively.
4   That which is present by chance and is, therefore, nonessential or that could be different than it is. By extension it signals the nonessential or optional character of any property or quality. This borrowing from logic occurs several times in the "Discourse of Laws."
5   Both the logic and the language of this passage correspond closely to Plato, *Laws* 875a.

affections and manners are depraved, and given over to unruly and unreasonable desires, there Laws be so necessary, that Heraclitus said, A City needed rather to defend their Laws, than Forts:[6] for without Laws no people can subsist; [510] without defenses, it is possible that they may: agreeing with Demosthenes's observation, who supposed Laws to be as the soul of a Commonwealth; for as a body without a soul, remains not; so a People without due administration of Laws, do wholly decline: but take people, as they are commonly mixed of the good, and worser sort, nay rather, more of the bad, than better composition, yet it will evidently appear, that Laws are so absolutely necessary, to restrain from ill, to confirm in good, to make a happy concord, and union in our civil conversation, to make such a distinction betwixt lawful, and exorbitant desires, as unlawful affections may not be colored with good appearances; that it cannot be denied, [511] that Laws be the only sinews of contracting people together, and not merely useful, but necessary.[7]

But in the exercise, and execution of Laws, such moderation is ever to be held, that it may appear rather to be used, as a preventing Physic, by way of example to warn others, that they fall not into the like danger, than out of a desire to afflict, or make miserable any private person: and therefore the conclusion of Tacitus is very observable:[8]

Pauca admodum vi tractata, quo ceteris quies esset [Tacitus, Annales 1.9.21–2]. In some few matters severity was used, by that means to cause quietness in the rest.

So that it is necessary in every Commonwealth to cut off offenders, as well for present safety, as prevention of further mis-

6   This famous statement derived from Diogenes Laertius, Lives of the Philosophers ix, 2, is collected and translated in Philip Wheelwright, Heraclitus (New York: Atheneum, 1964), p. 83, as follows: "The people should fight for their laws as for their city wall."

7   This thrice-used image of laws as sinews holding together the body politic may be borrowed from an earlier eclectic—Sir John Fortescue, De Laudibus Legum Anglie, or an even earlier source. The connection here would be more evident had S. B. Chrimes, the editor and translator of the best edition of De Laudibus (Cambridge, 1942), chosen to render the Latin nervus as "sinews" rather than "nerves" (see p. 31).

8   Worthy of mention.

chief, [512] which will be plain, if we will but observe the benefits that follow, and inconveniences that arise, if this exemplary Justice be not executed.

First, when any fact is unlawfully committed, there is no other satisfaction left to the world, or the party offended, than the punishment of the offender; which if it be not executed, Injustice were as well offered to the Public State, as to the private person of him who has suffered the injury.

Next, as it encourages honest men in their just and lawful actions; so it abates the insolence of others, who be only bridled with the fear of punishment; for otherwise the worst men by wickedest courses, were most likely to make great fortunes, [513] and to carry the greatest sway; which would so discourage men honestly disposed, that they would neither have will, nor power, nor confidence to labor for the public.

Thirdly, it banishes all presumption from such as think that their reputation and wealth, Riches, or Offices, can press down Justice, or make it incline to their purposes: for if these respects should prevail, judgment were merely inverted, and would not look upon the cause, but the Bribe; the right, but the power; the truth, but the greatness of the greater Adversary.

Again, it adds confidence to the poorer sort, when they see that equity, and not favor, procures the sentence, and so by this means are conserved from oppression. And if it were not for this, in what a miserable [514] case were these lower degrees of men subject to be trod under feet by their imperious Adversary, and then to have no means left for redress.

Fifthly, it is the greatest honor, and reputation, a Kingdom, or commonwealth can be ambitious of, and enjoy, to have Justice justly distributed, and people obedient to Laws; Justice guarding the people, by correcting and cutting off such as give ill example to the rest. And in what Commonwealth soever this is neglected, it breeds confusion amongst themselves, gives advantage to their enemies, and causes their disreputation[9] to spread through the world.

Next to the honor of a Kingdom, it is the safety of the King, who being reputed to be as the fountain of Justice, so

9 Evil reputation.

Justice keeps the fountain free from corruption, infection, or [515] danger, prescribing rules for fear it corrupt, ascribing Antidotes for fear of infection, and preserving his person, and reputation both from sensible, and insensitive danger: whereas if Laws be neglected, his person is more subject to the attempts of Traitors, his life to the tongues of malice and detraction, and his reputation to perpetual infamy.

And lastly, this is it, that enriches and secures the subject in all Kingdoms, gives him his right, protects him from wrong, increases commerce, and proclaims traffic throughout all the world: whereas if Justice were not duly administered, there would follow a diminution of our substances, a general disconsolation in our life, and a certain separation from all trade with strangers. And mark but narrowly, and [516] you shall seldom find that God ever blessed that Country, where Justice was either neglected, or abused.

Those therefore (if any such insensible creatures be) that dislike the restraint, and strive, and declaim against obedience to Laws (which may be truly termed the walls of government, and nations) they make themselves so contemptible, as no objection of theirs can be worthy the answering: for a general dissolution of Laws in a civil body, is the same with the convulsion of the sinews in a natural [body]; decay and dissolution, being the immediate, and unavoidable successors. And yet a man had better choose to live where no thing, than where all things be lawful: which is the reason why all men have thought it more dangerous, to live in an Anarchy [517] than under a Tyrant's government: for the violent desires of one, must necessarily be tied to particulars, in a multitude they are indefinite.

The first degree of goodness is obedience to Laws which be nothing else but virtue, and good order of life, reduced unto certain rules: and as reason has the predominant power in our natural bodies, so the body Politic cannot subsist without soul to animate,[10] to govern, to guide it, and that is Law proceeding from the reason, counsels, and judgment of wise men. For where Laws be wanting, there neither Religion, nor

10 The obsolete *inanimate* occurs in the original text as a verb indicating that the soul infuses the body with life.

life, nor society, can be maintained. There be three branches that men's Laws do spread themselves into, every one stricter than the other. The Law of Nature, which we enjoy in [518] common with all other living creatures. The Law of Nations, which is common to all men in general: and the Municipal Law of every Nation, which is peculiar and proper to this or that Country, and ours to us as Englishmen.

That of Nature, which is the ground or foundation of the rest, produces such actions amongst us, as are common to every living creature, and not only incident to men: as for example, the commixture of several sexes, which we call Marriage, generation, education, and the like; these actions belong to all living creatures as well as to us. The Laws of Nations be those rules which reason has prescribed to all men in general, and such as all Nations one with another do allow and observe for just. And lastly, the [519] Peculiar Laws of every Country, which mixed with the general Laws of all places, some particular ones of their own: and this is that which the Romans called amongst themselves, the Civil Law of their City, and is indeed in every Nation: the Municipal Laws of that Country, as it were Laws only created for those Climates, for those estates.[11]

Take away the power of Laws, and who is it that can say, This is my House, or my Land, or my money, or my goods, or call any thing that is his, his own. Therefore every man's state and fortune is more strengthened and confirmed by Laws, than by any will or power in those from whom we receive them; for whatsoever is left unto us by the Testament of another, it is impossible we should ever keep it [520] as our own, if Law restrained not others' claims, and confirmed them not unto us. In which respect, Laws be the strongest sinews of human society, helps for such as may be overborn,[12] and bridles to them that would oppress. So that we receive much more benefit from Laws in this kind, than from Nature; for whereas men be naturally affected and possessed with a violent heat of desires, and passions, and fancies, Laws restrain and draw them from those actions, and thoughts, that would precipitate to all

11 "Estates" can refer to worldly prosperity or to a form of government, among other possibilities.
12 Oppressed.

manner of hazards and ill, which natural inclination is prone enough unto; and do govern, direct, alter, dispose, and as it were bend them to all manner of virtuous and good actions.

Wherefore Laws be the true Physicians and preservers of our peaceable [521] life, and civil conversation, preventing those ill accidents that may happen, purging and taking away such as have broken forth, and sowing peace, plenty, wealth, strength, and all manner of prosperity amongst men. And for those things that be ill, but yet introduced by custom, severe and just Laws will readily correct; for the force and power of Law does easily dissolve an ill custom, though it [may] have been of long continuance: the excellency and praise of which Laws can never be better illustrated, than in that saying of Solomon:

Mandatum lucerna est; lex, lux, & via vitae, increpatio disciplinae.
The commandment is a lamp; and the law is light; and reproofs
of instruction, are the way of life [Prov. 6:23].

The dispensers and interpreters [522] of the Law, be the Magistrates and Judges, and all sorts and degrees of men whatsoever be tied and bound to the observance of the same. To this purpose, Solon being demanded, "What City was best governed?" answered, "That, wherein the City obeyed the Magistrate, and the Magistrate the Laws." And certainly that government is better, which uses set and firm Laws, though not all of the best sort, than that where the Laws be most perfect and exact, and yet not observed. Laws therefore ought to be the rulers of men, and not men the masters of Laws.

There is no doubt but that Laws were at the first invented, as well to give rules to the good, that they might know how to live peaceably and regularly one with another, as to repress the audacity of those [523] unbridled spirits, who, in despite of discipline and reason, do thrust themselves into all kinds of outrage and disorder; from which bad cause notwithstanding, according to the old rule, a good effect is produced: *ex malis moribus, bonae leges oriuntur.*[13] But the particular introductions of Laws, arise either from a pressing necessity, or a foreseeing and provisional carefulness of those that make them; these

13 "Good laws arise from bad customs."

proceed from providence, the other from some sense of evil. The impulsive causes[14] in the making of provisional[15] Laws, are either love of their Country, or desire of glory, or affectation[16] of popularity, or sometimes particular interest, and private respect; for it often happens, that a private good may have connection with the public. And the [524] sense of ill, decaying either by the increase of it, or a seeming to be destitute of remedy, is the cause, that where Laws are once forced, out of the sense of mischief, and inconvenience, they be for the most part grievous and immoderate; as on the other side, such as reason and providence do produce, are many times more specious[17] than useful. In the first, take away the spur and sense of ill, and it makes men in the constitution of Laws, to be careless and unwary; and in the other, if there be not continued a strong and constant affection, they commonly faint in the execution of them.

But in the meantime there is no doubt, that there are certain fountains of natural Justice and equity, out of which has been taken [525] and derived that infinite variety of Laws, which several people have apted[18] to themselves: and as several veins[19] and currents of water, have several qualities and tastes, in respect of the nature of that ground and soil, through which they flow and run: so these Laws and the virtue of them, which be fetched from an original fountain, receive a new kind of application, and tincture, in respect of the situation[20] of the Country, the genius[21] and nature of the people, the fashion

14   This seventeenth-century usage, now rare, denotes an originating or primary cause (*OED*, s.v. *impulsive*).

15   Both here and in the preceding sentence the meaning is not "temporary" but rather "characterized by or exhibiting careful foresight." This sentence is the *OED* example.

16   Pursuit.

17   Having an attractive appearance or character, calculated to make a favorable impression on the mind, but in reality devoid of the qualities apparently possessed.

18   To make fit or adapt.

19   Streamlets or rivulets.

20   The place, position, or location of a country in relation to its surroundings.

21   Prevalent feeling, opinion, sentiment, or taste; distinctive character, or spirit.

and form of public actions, divers accidents of the time, and sundry other occurrences, I will not stand[22] to repeat.[23] And in the making of Laws, wise men have always had these things in consideration:

1. First, the Common good, and benefit, for which they intend them, [526] and that requires that they should be both just and profitable. Now no law can be profitable, nor yet just, which is made for private and particular respects,[24] and not for the public good.

2. The persons to whom they be to be applied; that for the execution, and application of them, they be such as may be possible to be observed, and apt for the customs, places, and time, where, and when they be to be used.

3. The present course[25] of the State; what Laws there have been usually received, by what special ones it has been conserved, and by what new ones it may be assured: for one kind of care is not fit for all places, and Countries.

But Laws, when they are once made, ought very rarely to be changed: to which purpose the ancient position of wise men is not unworthy [527] the observing, "that nothing is to be changed in the Laws of a Commonwealth, which has a long time by these Laws preserved itself in good state and government:" and as Isidore well notes, after a Law is once made, "we ought not to judge of it, but according to it." And yet in these two cases the alteration of the Laws may turn to the better. 1. When by the changing of it the Law is made more perfect, more clear, more positive, more profitable. 2. When the condition of subjects and government is changed, there of necessity the Law must vary, according to the difference and diversity of the times and persons: for change and variation of Laws, are either by occasion of entertaining foreign customs, or some internal deficiencies, or excesses, according to the alteration of time. One [528] of these is so far from innovation, that it is

---

22 Pause.
23 Hobbes's image may be borrowed from Francis Bacon, *Of the Advancement of Learning*. See *The Works of Francis Bacon*, edited by James Spedding (London, 1859), vol. 3: 475.
24 Favors.
25 Habitual or ordinary manner of procedure: way, custom, practice.

altogether necessary: but that is not introducing of Laws by way of imitation of other people; it argues a desire of change, rather than any cause that is material. But on the other side, old and ancient customs, in respect of their very antiquity, do induce a kind of harshness, and breed satiety;[26] for the wilful retaining of a custom against the present reason of the time, is altogether unequal.

This is to be understood of temporary Laws, made and applied to new and several accidents. For the fundamental laws, upon which the fabric of a commonwealth and people be grounded and built, they in no case will admit innovation; neither are the other sort to be lightly altered, but where the [529] present custom of the time find them impertinent, and the State thinks them unuseful. To illustrate, in the same times, sometimes we see Laws mutable, and fit to be so: such as are made in time of war, peace does extinguish, and so on the contrary; agreeing with Livy speaking to this purpose:

Quae in pace lata sunt, plerumque bellum abrogat; quae in bello, pax; ut in navis administratione, alia in secunda, alia in adversa tempestate usui sunt.[27]

And although change of Laws be sometimes necessary, it ought notwithstanding to be done with a great deal of caution: but yet it must be confessed, that time, of all things is the greatest innovator, and therefore wilfully to prescribe the continuance of an old Law, in respect of antiquity, the face of the world [530] and affairs being changed, is indeed an introduction of novelty; for the pressure of the use of it, urging and setting it only forth with the grace of antiquity, if notwithstanding it be opposite or incongruous to the present times and government, makes that old Law, if practiced, to fall, and be converted into a new and unreasonable custom.

Now for my judgment concerning the use of Laws, I think

26 The sense here may be that ancient customs can bring unequal satisfactions to different people if the customs are not adjusted to changing circumstances.

27 Livy, *Ab Urbe Condita* 34.6.6.1–3. "Those laws which are made in peace are extinguished fully by war, those made in war, peace kills; as in the handling of a ship, some rules are used when the wind is in the sails, and others when sailing against the wind."

this, that as the use of much Physic and divers Physicians, argue the abundance of humors,[28] and diseases; so the multiplicity and number of Laws, be manifest signs of a diseased and distempered Commonwealth. And therefore to follow the similitude, as in diseases new experiments be dangerous, where those [531] that be ancient and approved may serve; so new Laws be needless, when the maladies of the Republic may be cured by the old: for it is a thing both unequal and unjust to ensnare the people with [a] multitude of Laws.

Law and Reason are twins, the absence of one, is the deformity of the other; being in a kind *convertibilia*,[29] and inseparable. That common reason we have engrafted in our natures, is a Law, directing what we are to do, forbidding the contrary, according to Cicero:

Eadem ratio cum est in hominis mente confirmata, & confecta, lex est.[30]

For Law is nothing but reason dilated[31] and applied upon several occasions and accidents, the comprehension of reason and Law, as of public enormities, and necessities, for [532] which they be severally, at several times made, being infinite. The disease commonly in our knowledge, having the priority of the remedy. And thus the reverence, and duty we owe to Laws, is nothing else but obedience to reason, which is the begetter, corrector, and preserver, of the very Laws themselves: those therefore who will not obey them, do come more near the nature of Brutes and Savages, than men endowed with reason: but I go on.

If a reason be demanded why all Countries do differ, and vary so much in their customs, and Laws, I answer, that it proceeds from the custom of the first inhabitants. As we may see where there are several plantations by one people, they severally give different orders, and customs, [533] according to the intent and purpose of the first Planters, and according to the

28 Mental disposition as determined by the proportion of bodily humors (fluids).
29 Capable by nature of being converted, the one into the other.
30 Cicero, *De Legibus* 1.6.18. "That very reason, when it is confirmed and established in the mind of man, is law."
31 Enlarged or extended.

necessity, and end of the present Plantation, as may be observed in the different Constitutions, and Laws, in our two late Plantations, of Virginia, and the Bermudas.[32] And though, I confess, that these original customs, may in time be altered, upon several occasions, divers changes of government, as in the Roman State, or upon conquest, as with us; yet I doubt not, but that some relics of the old customs would remain to perpetuity, if a people be not wholly extirpated. I should now punctually search the several Authors, and Inventors of Laws, amongst different Nations, together with their divers oppositions, and emulations,[33] one with another, [534] but that would be too long, and uncertain; I will therefore only in a word touch the original, and growth of Law amongst the Romans, as being more certainly known, and of larger extent.

You must understand that at the first they had no other set Law, than the will, and commandments of their Princes. That government being changed, and so their constitutions extinct, the people were then governed by precedent, and custom, without any direct, and written Law; but that continued not many years. Then the law of the 12 Tables succeeded, which the Romans, in respect of their own defects, had borrowed from the Grecians: and these, as in Laws it commonly happens, being subject to dispute, were forced to be reconciled, and decided, by the [535] authority, and arguments of the most great, grave, and learned men, which afterwards being collected, and gathered together, became a kind of volume, and body of Law, and so afterwards, before the Commonwealth was subverted, received by divers men, in sundry ages, several additions: but after the government was Monarchical, the present Emperors did add to the old, or confirm or abolish them, according to their own will, and power. And all together is that which is commonly known by the name of the civil Law, and because it continues to be the most practical, and generally received Law of the world, and that though all Countries have Municipal Laws of their own, yet this Law in every place carries some sway, and authority, in some places [536] more, and in

32   See Malcolm (1981), p. 321, for evidence that these references may date the composition of this discourse to within five years of its 1620 publication.
33   Endeavors to equal or excel the achievements of others.

some less, and that an aspersion is cast upon the ground, and foundation of our Laws, in being different and contrary to the original beginning of the civil Law, I will briefly parallel them together; wherein if any do not find so punctual an agreement as he expects, let him remember that the nature of a comparison, implies but a similitude, and affinity of one thing to another, and not a total and absolute agreement.[34]

The Law which the Romans used, and so we, is either written, or not written. Those that were written, says Justinian, were of these kinds. 1. *Lex,* and that is such a Law as was made by the people, but first propounded by the Senate. Such are those Laws with us, as are confirmed by the lower House of Parliament, [537] and propounded by the higher. 2. *Plebiscitum,* and such were the Laws made by the whole people (the order of Patricians excepted) and offered to their consideration by the Tribune; like those Laws that be approved by the Commons in our Parliament, and propounded by the Speaker. 3. *Senatus consulta,* and those were such Laws as were ordained by the power and authority of the Senate, to which we may resemble[35] the consultations and directions of the King's Council, and the Decrees of the Star-chamber. 4. *Principium Placita,* which were Constitutions[36] appointed by the Sovereign power of the Prince; some of them being personal, and not exemplary; others more public, of which kind with us be all the King's Edicts, and Proclamations, of what kind soever. 5. *Magistratuum* [538] *Edicta,* as the commandments of the Generals in the Field, Governors of Provinces, and the prime Magistrates in great Cities: like as with us is that power which is deputed to the Deputy of Ireland, the Presidents of York, and Wales, the Lieutenants of every Shire, and the Jurisdiction of Magistrates, according to their particular customs, privileges, and immunities, in the great Cities, and Corporations of this Kingdom. And lastly, [6.] *Responsa Prudentium,* which were the Judgments and opinions of such as were appointed to be

---

34 The seven-point comparison that Hobbes develops here reappears in a slightly expanded and rearranged form near the end of *Leviathan,* chapter 26.
35 Compare or liken.
36 Decrees, ordinances, or regulations.

Judges, and expounders of the Law: and just of that kind be the resolutions of our Judges, which in writing be delivered unto us, by the name of Reports, and Cases.

Laws unwritten amongst the Romans, [539] were such as custom had introduced, and yet never suffered contradiction by a Positive Law. Such Traditions as they had received touching the ancient manner, and form of government of their Ancestors, in precedent times; and of this nature with us is our common Law, grounded much upon custom.

And the reason why these ancient customs may be collected[37] to be of so great force, is, because always before their approbation it is to be conceived, that they had passed all censures[38] for necessary, and to be without offense: and so having received this facile approbation, are allowed, and most religiously kept; for Laws of the greatest weight, and consequence, which occasioned Cicero to write,

> *ante suam memoriam, & morem ipsum patrium,* [540] *praestantes viros adhibuisse, & veterum morem, ac maiorum instituta, excellentes viros retinuisse.*[39]

And believing Dionysius's testimony, Romulus in the first foundation of the Republic, did think to strengthen, and confirm it more, with Laws unwritten, than written; peradventure being of the same opinion Demosthenes notes of Lycurgus, who would not write his Laws, but to have them more public, and better known, would leave them only engraven in the memory of his Citizens.

But more precisely to distinguish betwixt Law and Custom, that the terms, as well as matter, may be understood, you must understand, that where any form, or Law, has had any long continuance in practice, without any [541] known Author, it

---

37 Used this way before an infinitive, it suggests a logical gathering. Concluded, inferred, deduced, etc.

38 As above, it may indicate criticisms, or even formal, judicial judgments. In this case, it may specifically refer to the review of the ancient Roman censors.

39 Cicero *De Re Publica* 5.1.7–10. Cicero's text reads: *Itaque ante nostram memoriam et mos ipse patrius praestantes viros adhibebat, et veterem morem ac maiorum instituta retinebant excellentes viri.* The Loeb translation reads: "Thus, before our own time, the customs of our ancestors produced excellent men, and eminent men preserved our ancient customs and the institutions of their forefathers."

then receives the name of an ancient custom, or *mos Maiorum:* which though in name, and Title it differ from a Law, yet in power, and authority, it is the same: which Ulpian confirmed when he said,

> *Diuturna consuetudo pro Iure, et Lege, in his quae non ex scripto descendunt, observari solet.*[40]

And there is great reason for it, because Laws are in esteem, and authority with us, for no other reason, but in respect they have had the reputation to be allowed, and made by the Judgment of the people. Then full as meritoriously do those Laws deserve esteem, which all men have approved for necessary, without any prescript,[41] or rule; and this is the reason which makes our common Law originally [542] grounded upon ancient customs, of equal power and authority with our Statutes.

FINIS.

---

40 *Digest* 1.3.33.1–2. "Among these which are not promulgated in writing, long-lasting custom is usually observed as right and law."
41 Ordinance or regulation, thing prescribed.

PART THREE

HOBBES AND THE BEGINNINGS OF MODERN POLITICAL THOUGHT

HOBBES AND THE BEGINNINGS OF MODERN POLITICAL THOUGHT

Arlene W. Saxonhouse

INTRODUCTION

T HERE ARE MANY WAYS to read the three *Discourses:* for what they tell us about the social and religious life of the English aristocrat in the early decades of the seventeenth century, for what they tell us about where people traveled comfortably (and not so comfortably), for an understanding of the development of the literary genres of the essay and the discourse. Our purpose here, though, is briefly to explore the political ideas of the author whose later writings are masterpieces of political theory and whose work gave rise, in part, to the principles underlying modern liberalism. The *Discourses,* by offering us Hobbes's early reflections on the political questions that will engage him for the rest of his life, help us understand the challenges that confronted those moving from a medieval, religiously focused worldview to modern, secular models built on an infinite universe that is at the foundation of liberal political thought.[1]

The *Discourses*—admittedly immature when compared to Hobbes's mature writings and certainly inconsistent at times—point to the central concern of modern thought: how to identify the secular sources of a political power that might provide for security and stability in a world of constant flux. The "Discourse upon the Beginning of Tacitus" faces this challenge directly while the "Discourse of Laws" explores how to integrate a legal system based on human rather than divine reason into a political system founded on human choice and will. As such, these *Discourses* not only offer insights into the intellectual development of Thomas Hobbes; they also enlighten us about the beginning of liberalism itself and the contradictions that this new political outlook must address.

One of the most salient features of the *Discourses* is the affinity they reveal between Hobbes and Niccolò Machiavelli.[2] Leo Strauss is not the only theorist to suggest that the modern

1 Koyré (1959:vi) perhaps most elegantly describes this transformation in the pattern of thought that reached its apex in the seventeenth century: "[T]he destruction of the cosmos and the geometrization of space, that is the substitution for the conception of the world as a finite and well-ordered whole, in which the spatial structure embodied a hierarchy of perfection and value, that of an indefinite or even infinite universe no longer united by the identity of its elements and basic components." See also Greenleaf (1964).

2 That Hobbes uses the discourse form and title for his reflections is itself interesting; the discourse had not yet become a popular literary genre in English literature by the time Hobbes was writing. In contrast, the essay, the form which comprises the first half of the *Horae Subsecivae*, had quickly taken hold in England in the late sixteenth and early seventeenth centuries, most prominently in Bacon's writing. Among a variety of other definitions, the *OED* describes the discourse as "a dissertation, treatise, sermon, homily, or the like" and refers to a 1581 text. The use of discourse in the actual title of a work occurs in 1575: "A brief Discourse off the Troubles . . . abowte the Booke off Common Prayer and Ceremonies," and, of course, it appears in the discourse found not to be by Hobbes that appears in the *Horae Subsecivae*, the "Discourse against Flatterie," which was published separately and anonymously in 1611 (Pollard 1946, no. 6906), but the form was not nearly as familiar as the essay at this time. By the end of the century the discourse is a common form, especially for theological treatises. The most familiar work written in the discourse form at the time that Hobbes was writing his own discourses would have been the *Discorsi* of Machiavelli.

political perspective emerged in Machiavelli's work a century before Hobbes wrote the *Discourses*. As he states in his introduction to the second American edition of his book on Hobbes: "Hobbes appeared to me [at the time of the first edition] as the originator of modern political philosophy. This was an error: not Hobbes, but Machiavelli, deserves this honor" (1952, xv). This self-correction, though, provides us with a key to understand the novelty of Hobbes's human-centered world where political order is imposed against, rather than in conformity with, nature. These modest writings allow us now to see Hobbes standing at the watershed of modern political thought well before he brought methods of geometry or physics to his analysis of political events.[3] The *Discourses,* by allowing us to read the "pre-scientific" Hobbes, enable us to speculate briefly on the impact that the scientific turn had on Hobbes's political thought. The interest that he develops later in the scientific method and the study of bodies in motion is an accretion to his motivating interest in things political displayed in the *Discourses.* It is, without doubt, an accretion that allows him to formulate in novel and important ways his mature ideas concerning political life, but it does not significantly alter the primary concerns and orientations that he developed as a young man.

The *Discourses* should not be read simply as the immature expression of ideas later presented more fully by Hobbes, for they reveal how the ideas themselves were generated. At the birth of modern political thought is Hobbes's insight that political order can emerge as the result of human rather than divine efforts. In the *Discourses* he analyzes the efforts of the prince—the one skilled in policy—and of the lawmakers to bring about order. Instead of accepting the traditional view and assuming an inherent natural order that needs to be discovered and implemented through the laws and the institutions of the political community, Hobbes reinterprets the past and introduces new theories about the present by pointing to political orders dependent on human will. Here, in his writings

3   The *Discourses* also show Hobbes interested in these questions of order well before the crises of the English civil war made even more vivid the need to identify the new sources of political authority.

at the beginning of the seventeenth century, Hobbes describes how the prince—the new prince—makes certain critical choices and thereby replaces chaos with order.

The *Discourses* suggest a serious Hobbes who is struggling with some of the same questions that will engage him when he writes *Leviathan* some thirty years later. We see him in the *Discourses* working to free himself from the conventional thought of the time, not always successfully or consistently. But the incompatibility of the old worldview and the demands of a political world without foundations in religion or precedent pose for him challenges that he acknowledges here and that his later work will attempt to resolve.

A DISCOURSE UPON THE BEGINNING OF TACITUS

The political concern for defining and determining the origins of political communities and authority within them drives the *Discourses* and especially the discourse devoted to the first four paragraphs of Tacitus' *Annales*. The study of human history looks to origins rather than to ends, to causes rather than to conclusions, to examples rather than to precepts (Strauss 1952, chap. 6). Science, as the study of causes or origins, later helps clarify for Hobbes how to analyze political questions, but the young Hobbes turned originally to history to explore the causes of political order and disorder in pre-Christian Rome.

In some ways Tacitus can be described as the Roman Thucydides, and Hobbes's translation of Thucydides published some ten years later continues his interest in historical writing from the ancient world.[4] But Thucydides provides Hobbes with

4 It is unclear when Hobbes decided to publish his translation of Thucydides. In his verse autobiography he says of his readings of the classical authors, poets, historians, playwrights, both Greek and Roman, that Thucydides pleased him the most. (LW 1: lxxxviii.) This was during the time that he enjoyed the friendship and leisure entailed in acting as the tutor of the William Cavendish who was to be the second earl of Devonshire. In the Preface to the Reader introducing his translation, Hobbes remarks about it: "After I had finished it, it lay long by me; and other reasons taking place, my desire to communicate it ceased" (Hobbes 1975, 8–9).

quite a different window on political life. Thucydides' re-counting of the Peloponnesian War and the transformation of the Athenian polity during that war gives insight into the causes of war, its execution, and its consequences. But apart from its introductory chapters, or so-called "archaeology," on which Hobbes does not comment directly in his own introductory remarks, Thucydides' history does not address the issue of foundations. The beginning of the *Annales* poses just that question and enables Hobbes to question the causes of order before he turns to Thucydides to study the causes of disorder. Hobbes is clearly already asking these questions about causes, well before he adopts the more systematic models concerning causes in the natural world that arise from his interactions with the emerging scientific communities of the seventeenth century.[5]

According to the standard biographies and his own accounts written late in life,[6] Hobbes spent the early decades of the seventeenth century in pleasurable travel and light pursuits, not in serious philosophical study (LW: I.xii–xiv; I. lxxxviii). Hobbes reports that after coming back from his first trip abroad,[7] he turned to the historians and the poets, with the frequent use of grammatical commentaries, in order to be able to compose moderately good Latin. Aubrey supports Hobbes's presentation of himself when he comments: "Before Thucydides, he spent two years reading romances and playes,

5 Numerous scholars have focused on one influence or another as the basis for Hobbes's full philosophical and political system. Whether it be the "resolutive-deductive" system of Watkins (1965), or the geometric method of Goldsmith (1966), or the aristocratic sensibilities noted by Strauss ([1936] 1952) and Thomas (1965), or the impact of reading Descartes (Tuck 1988), any such assessments of the influences on Hobbes's thought will need to return to these early *Discourses* and address the defining influences that may surface from a careful reading of these writings.

6 Aubrey (1898, 395) affirms that the prose autobiography is by Hobbes, noting in his introduction: "This was the draught that Mr. Hobbs did leave in my hands, which he sent for about two years before he died, and wrote that which is printed by Dr. Richard Blackburn."

7 Noel Malcolm (1984) provides new evidence that this trip to the Continent took place from the autumn of 1614 to the spring of 1615, rather than in 1610 as had originally been conjectured by most scholars.

which he haz often repented and said that these two years were lost of him—perhaps he was mistaken. For it might furnish him with copie of words" (1898: 351).[8]

Hobbes's sentence-by-sentence commentary on Tacitus' *Annales* follows a tradition that was established in the sixteenth century and continued well into the seventeenth century. Hobbes's decision to comment only on the first four paragraphs of the *Annales* makes his analysis of Tacitus' history unique; it indicates the questions that engage him and displays his early efforts at providing answers to those questions. Through his analysis of Tacitus, Hobbes offers a series of Machiavellian maxims as guides for the founders of political orders. In doing so, he also demonstrates his commitment to discovering the sources of political order.

Tacitus, the Roman historian who detailed in clipped Latin prose the iniquities of the Roman emperors of the first century A.D., became especially popular in the sixteenth century. His *Annales* and *Histories* were published, translated, commented upon, and the commentaries were translated and commented upon in turn. The first English translation of Tacitus appeared in 1591 and within the next forty-nine years this translation went through five more editions (Womersley 1991, 313). As one scholar notes, between 1580 and 1700 more than 150 authors wrote commentaries on Tacitus, with most of those coming in the first half of the seventeenth century (Burke 1969, 150). Tacitus' popularity rested in part on a reading of his works as tirades against the corruption of monarchical power and thus as a call for the republican form of

8   We do know that Hobbes's modest description of his intellectual concerns prior to the publication of the Thucydides translation is not quite accurate, since during that time he was translating letters written in Italian by Fra Fulgenzio Micanzio, a Venetian, who had begun a lengthy correspondence with the second earl of Devonshire. The letters, dating from 1615 to 1628, contain detailed discussions of the political conditions in Venice, as well as extensive commentaries on the works of Bacon. Two manuscripts of these letters are known to us, one in the library at Chatsworth, the other in the British Museum (add. MS 11,309). Neither of these is written in Hobbes's hand, but the manuscript at Chatsworth has on the flyleaf, in Hobbes's writing: "Translated out of the original Italian Letters by Th: Hobbes Secretary to ye Lord Cavendish." Malcolm (1984) and Sommerville (1992, 76–78) discuss these letters at some length.

government that had been lost when Augustus established the Principate. For many of these commentators, Tacitus served as the basis for their antityrannical tracts that explored justifications for rebellion against evil kings, a theme that the Protestant Reformation had brought to the forefront of political thinking.

In addition, Tacitus emerged as a cover for Machiavellian themes. While Machiavelli wrote his commentary on the beginning of Livy's history (or the first ten books of it), he also uses Tacitean aphorisms at critical points.[9] To cite Machiavelli directly—the incarnation of evil from whom, according to the stage productions of the time, the devil learned his tricks (Raab 1964)—in the sixteenth or even seventeenth century was dangerous, though a few like Bacon showed no hesitation or worry about incurring the unfavorable notice such attention to and respect for the Florentine might entail (Orsini 1936). To cite Tacitus, however, entailed no such danger. Justus Lipsius, the Dutch author who edited the authoritative edition of Tacitus in the sixteenth century, wrote his *Politicorum, sive, Civilis doctrinae libris sex* relying heavily on Tacitus. Indeed, the work is almost an unending and uninterrupted string of Tacitean aphorisms. As Lipsius' English translator noted in 1594: "Gentle reader, if thou please, thou mayest with one view, behold those authors, from whom this discourse is gathered. Amongst the which Cornelius Tacitus has the preeminence, being recited extraordinarily" (Lipsius 1594 [spelling modernized]).[10] Authors such as Giuseppe Toffanin

9 Though Machiavelli seldom cites Tacitus directly, there are some key passages from Tacitus in Machiavelli's texts, e.g., compare Chapter 13 of *The Prince* and Tacitus' *Annales* 13.19; see also Machiavelli's *Discourses* 1.10 where Machiavelli lifts a paragraph directly from the introduction to Tacitus' *Histories;* compare *Discourses* 1.29 and *Histories* 4.3, and see especially *Discourses* 3.19 where Tacitus is cited as the author who feels that severity is more important for a ruler than gentleness. Mansfield (1979, 373–86) comments extensively on this passage, as does Strauss (1958, 160–65). Womersley (1991, 316) goes so far as to argue that "a powerful knowledge of Machiavelli's *The Prince*" enabled a sixteenth-century translator of Tacitus to fill "up the blanks and spaces left by his source."

10 According to Hamilton (1978, 450) this book was in the Hardwick Library where Hobbes would have had frequent access to it as a member of the Cavendish household.

([1921] 1972) have argued that there were two separate strands of Tacitism; Toffanin called them the black and the red. The former entailed drawing republican lessons from Tacitean aphorisms, the latter Machiavellian ones from many of the same aphorisms. Though Toffanin's claims are now seen as exaggerated (Burke, 1969), a pattern does exist in the sixteenth century of aligning Tacitus with Machiavelli as well as with antityrannical authors. In one version, Tacitus is the exponent of Machiavellian themes of "reason of state" and offers a catalogue of the crimes necessary to preserve whatever regime is in power. In the other version, Tacitus points to the dangers of tyranny, and his stories of the violence and immorality of the Roman princes seem to justify rebellions against tyrants.[11] So popular was Tacitus in England and on the Continent that a whole school of anti-Tacitus literature appeared as well.[12]

While others found in Tacitus a way to express their views on the political events of the day, Hobbes's Tacitus is primarily a resource for explaining political foundations. Hobbes says little about "reasons of state," less about the dangers of tyranny, and nothing about justifications for rebellion; rather, he examines the account of Augustus' ascension to and assertion of political power to illuminate the origins of states and the challenge of political foundations. The section on which Hobbes comments is the very brief introduction to the *Annales* in which Tacitus quickly describes the transition from the Republic to the Principate under Augustus. Most of the lengthy *Annales* and what concerned most of the others who used Tacitus as a storehouse of aphorisms relates the actions of the series of princes who followed Augustus—Tiberius, Claudius, Nero, and on down the line of abhorrent rulers. Hobbes's fo-

11 Womersley (1991, 326–27) cites an edition of the Huguenot *Vindiciae Contra Tyrannos* published in Basel that appeared bound with a Latin translation of *The Prince*, with the explanation that Machiavelli is the counsellor of the "true prince" and not of tyrants. As such, Machiavelli can help identify the false princes who must be overthrown. In general, Womersley clearly explains the relation between Machiavelli and Tacitus and the use of these authors to justify rebellion.

12 Bywaters and Zwicker (1989) follow the pro- and anti-Tacitean movements in England in particular.

cus is directly on the institutional origins of the Principate rather than its sordid development in the reigns of subsequent rulers.

Hobbes's fascination with Augustus as he appears in the brief introductory remarks by Tacitus focuses on Augustus' role as a new prince in a new state (255, 257)[13] who is confronted by the difficulties of asserting authority and winning the support of his subjects. A new prince in a state that was once free faces the challenges engendered by making enemies of those who were once eager for change and must now settle for what is. To quote Machiavelli: "But the difficulties reside in the new principality. . . . Its instability arises in the first place from a natural difficulty that exists in all new principalities. This is that men willingly change their masters in the belief that they will fare better: this belief makes them take up arms against him, in which they are deceived because they see later by experience that they have done worse."[14] It is precisely this challenge that confronts Augustus. He is not able to turn, as a king of the seventeenth century could, to foundations in divine right.

James I, writing about the time the *Discourses* were composed, expresses at least the official theory of the source of political authority. In a passage addressed to his son, he admonishes him: "Learn to know and love God, to whom ye have a double obligation; first for that he made you a man; next, for that he made a little God to sit on His Throne, and rule over other men" (McIlwain 1918, 12; spelling and punctuation modernized). In the verse introduction to *Basilikon Doron*, James portrays again the divine source of political power: "God gives not kings the style of gods in vain,/ For on his throne his scepter do they sway;/ And as their subjects ought them to obey,/ So kings should fear and serve their God again" (McIlwain 1918, 3).

Augustus cannot rely on such divine support in his asser-

---

13 The page numbers refer to the original pagination of the 1620 edition of the *Horae Subsecivae* and are included in Hobbes's text printed above.

14 Machiavelli (1985), *The Prince*, Chapter 3 (Mansfield translation, 7–8). On the availability of Machiavelli's writings, see Praz ([1928] 1973) and Raab (1964, chap. 2).

tion of political power over the Roman state, but neither is he restrained by any such limits as James articulates for his son. Instead, neither supported nor restrained by a divine order, Augustus uses his own skills—or in the loaded term of the time, "policy" (Raab 1965, 78)—to transform the chaotic liberty of the Republic to the ordered model of the Principate. Thus we learn of, and are urged to admire, Augustus' efforts to root out the "stout patriots" who, unapt to bend to the needs of a new regime governed by a new prince, wanted to defend liberty. In good Machiavellian fashion Hobbes asserts that even if they had been allies and members of Augustus' own faction, they could not "be left alive" (264). Such "stubborn companions," had they not been gotten "rid of" (265), would have demanded participation in the new authority and thus they would have divided sovereignty. The rest will "accept the present with security, rather than strive for the old, with danger" (267). Augustus knew he had to "extinguish" the fiercer men and allure the gentler sort.

The Hobbesian message here—whether we see it as building on Machiavellian beneficent violence or as foreshadowing *Leviathan*—is that before the construction of the state neither vice nor virtue exist. The language of *Leviathan* 13 is foreshadowed in these sections of the *Discourses:* "Where there is no common power, there is no law: where no law, no injustice. . . . Justice and injustice are none of the faculties neither of body nor mind." And as Hobbes points out in discussing the regicides who killed the last Roman king as the prelude to the founding of the Republic: "But I shall never think otherwise of it than thus; *Prosperum et felix scelus virtus vocatur*" (228).

Likewise, in language that again recalls Machiavelli, Hobbes notes that traditional virtues are vices and vices are virtues. Liberality costs a country liberty (258) and as a variety of stories from Rome illustrate, generosity leads to absolute sovereignty (259–60).[15] The standards for virtues and vices as traditionally understood do not limit the founding of states, because there are no such standards before such foundings. For the modern authors like Hobbes and Machiavelli the central human task of political founding precedes the moral or-

15   See *The Prince,* Chapter 16 in particular, and Orwin (1978).

der. The latter comes only as the result of a political foundation, not as the prior limit on its construction. The security
that a James I might have felt with the backing of divine authority for his own ascension to political power and his position as king entailed as well the moral limits on his actions
that such a backing required. The open world that Machiavelli
envisioned and that Hobbes recalls in his praises for Augustus
allows for a freedom of political action denied to those whose
security comes from the nature of God and not from their own
efforts. Hobbes emphasizes in this discourse the openness at
the moment of founding; Tacitus' *Annales* chronicles how subsequent rulers failed to use this openness effectively, earning
moral condemnation from their contemporaries and later
writers and being unable to provide the political stability Augustus achieved at the start of the Principate.

Hobbes, in his reflections on the fall of the kings which
led to the establishment of the Roman Republic, finds fault
not with the form of monarchical government that was overthrown in the name of liberty, but with the private excesses of
the king's son, excesses which offended and threatened otherwise obedient subjects. The limits on the monarch suggested
here do not come from natural law or divine restraints but
from what we find later in chapter 30 of *Leviathan* and can
call "monarchical prudence." As Hobbes argues in his early
discourse: "It is not the [form of] government [in this case,
monarchy] but the abuse that makes the alteration be termed
Liberty" (229). Monarchy is approved insofar as it retains the
support of the king's subjects, not insofar as it follows any
moral principles of political authority. It can retain the alle-
giance of its subjects, however, only insofar as the regime respects their private interests. When the king's son rapes the
wife of one of the leading subjects, such an action may well
bring about revolution. The issue is not the right or wrong of
the action in an absolute sense; the issue thus framed is the
degree to which the ruler's acts support or hinder the security
of the political authority, be it aristocratic, republican, or monarchical.[16]

16 This section of the *Discourses* where Hobbes praises monarchical rule suggests difficulties with certain of Strauss's conclusions concerning Hobbes's

As this discourse makes clear, the instability of regimes dominates Hobbes's thought long before England is racked by civil war. The challenge he sees for political leaders is how to ensure a stability that does not reside in the natural order of things by founding a regime in which the people "apply themselves wholly to the Arts of service, whereof obsequiousness is the chief" (307). The Roman Republic, with its exaltation of liberty, offers a model of the instability that emerges from equality, where men "study no more the Art of commanding which had been heretofore necessary for any Roman Gentleman, when the rule of the whole might come to all of them in their turns" (307). Hobbes drawing on Tacitus' two brief phrases describing the beginning of the Republic ("Liberty and the Consulship Lucius Brutus brought in" and "The Decemviri passed not two years" [227, 231]) points out that the people, freed from the rule of kings, "grew perplexed at every inconvenience, and shifted from one form of government to another." They are like a sick man with a fever who, he says, often tosses "to and fro in his bed" (231). It was a regime that loved change and a variety of government (234). Such tossing and such shifting bring on civil war, what Hobbes, long before he himself has experienced it, calls "the worst thing that can happen to a State" (239). It is the liberty of the Republic that

---

early thought ([1936] 1952). In particular, Strauss argues that Hobbes at first emphasized an "affinity between monarchy and paternal authority" (62) and that it was only his increased interest in representation that led to a change of view from monarchy as the best natural state to the best artificial state. While references to the patrimonial justifications for monarchy do appear in Hobbes's *Elements of Law* (*EW* II. v. 3) and *De Cive* (II. x. 3), Strauss's claim that "Hobbes came only gradually to cast them aside and . . . at first he considered [patrimonial] monarchy to be the only natural form of authority" (60) does not find support in the *Discourses*. Similarly, Strauss argues that Hobbes only gradually moved to a "wholehearted rejection of the idea of a mixed constitution. His original opinion will have been that the absolute monarch is by no means obliged, but would do well, to set up an aristocratic or democratic council, and thus unite the advantages of monarchy with those of aristocracy or democracy" (68). Such a claim finds no support in this discourse, although Hobbes would have had ample opportunity to praise a mixed regime such as that found in the Roman Republic, the primary model for the mixed form. Instead, from his earliest writings, Hobbes is firm in his presentation of the advantages of monarchical rule—but not monarchical rule based on the analogy with divine rule over the universe or paternal rule in the family.

allows for the chaos, and only after "the Commonwealth relinquished her liberty, and confessed herself subdued" (250) does the order of the state emerge.

Augustus did not make the same mistakes the founders of the Republic made. Once he established himself in a position of power, through policy, through purgings, through the manipulation of opinions and desires, indeed through violence as well, only then could the populace of Rome enjoy the "sweetness of ease" and only then could they welcome the "vacancy of War" (260). Augustus, not temporary leaders like Cinna or Sulla, knew how to use violence to transform the chaos of the Republic and civil war to a regime that lasted more than a year or two. He transformed a people once accustomed to equality to a people who now realize that "striving for equality, is not the best of their game, but obedience, and waiting on the command of him that had power to raise, or keep them low at his pleasure" (306), and a people as well who recognize that in the "subject of a Monarch, obedience is the greatest virtue" (307). Cinna and Sulla, the usurpers of political power in the early years of the first century while Rome was still a republic, failed "to have mollified or extinguished the fiercer, allured the gentler sort." Thus, they could not assure "to themselves by politic provisions" what "they had obtained by arms" (235).

In contrast, the story of Augustus' founding becomes in Hobbes's hands a "mirror of princes" as he identifies in Machiavellian fashion the necessary first principles of a stable political regime. What might in the traditional discourse be considered personal virtues are less relevant than knowledge concerning the crafts or arts of politics. And Hobbes makes clear that virtue is no assurance of a good ruler: "though he might prove no ill man, he might be nevertheless an ill governor" (297). In particular, we might note Hobbes's extended gloss on the Tacitean phrase "with the title of Prince" which in Hobbes's hands turns into a discourse on the priority of what appears to be over what is, on the prince's need to control minds and wills as "the noblest and surest command of all other" (254). As he notes: "Most men receive as great content from Title, as substance" (240), and "in a multitude, seeming things, rather than substantial, make impression" (241). Augustus, Hobbes explains, knew that the aggrandizement of personal power does not stir men to sedition as "insolent titles" do, and thus he chose a title that would not remind them of their kings. "To give them then content in words, which cost him neither money, nor labor, he thought no dear bargain" (241). Later in the story, Hobbes comments on Augustus' willingness to shed the title "triumvir" since the title itself would evoke recollections of the civil wars, "and a new Prince ought to avoid those names of authority, that rub upon the Subjects' wounds, and bring hatred, and envy" (255).

Hobbes's assertion that a founder must rely on appearances for the security of his position is a euphemism for a ruler's need to deceive. For writers of this time, chapter 18 of *The Prince* captured the heart of Machiavelli's teaching. "In What Mode Faith Should be Kept by Princes" Machiavelli asked, and in answer he makes clear that faith need not be kept; rather, the prince must remember that "men are so simple and so obedient that he who deceives will always find someone who will let himself be deceived" and that "Men in general judge more by their eyes than by their hands. . . . Everyone sees how you appear, few touch what you are."[17]

Sixteenth- and seventeenth-century Europe believed that Machiavelli's approbation of deceit captured the central message of his teaching (Raab 1965), and Hobbes, in this most Machiavellian of discourses, does not hesitate to recommend deceit when it is necessary for political foundings. Augustus "turns to dissimulation, which was in those times held an inseparable accident of a politic Prince" (285). The wise prince does not take away "all the show of their liberty at one blow." Rather, he gradually eases his subjects into accepting their servitude (261). No apologies are offered—just admiration for Augustus' success at political founding. Evaluating the qualities of Agrippa—the prince who would not become emperor because of his untimely death—Hobbes notes Agrippa's lack of just those skills that he finds in Augustus: "the Art of conforming to times, and places, and persons . . . to contain and dissemble his passions, and purposes; and this was then thought the chief Art of government" (297). It is almost as if he were

17   Mansfield translation, pp. 70–71.

quoting from the twenty-fifth chapter of *The Prince* when he taxes Agrippa for lacking these qualities. In contrast to Agrippa, Tiberius (who does succeed Augustus) knows "best of all men how to dissemble his vices" (317).

In Hobbes's later writings, he will not urge on his rulers the personal exercise of deception; it will not be necessary. With the exercise of complete authority and with an epistemology that questions the existence of any truth outside deductions from first principles, dissimulation will have no meaning and cannot be central to the ensuring of political power. Control of public opinion, however, is crucial. The sovereign who neglects to define words for his subjects will find himself displaced by those who claim to have definitions for such terms as "justice" and "liberty" that are superior to or more attractive than those of the sovereign. "The common people's mind, unless they be tainted with dependence on the potent, or scribbled over with the opinions of their doctors, are like clean paper, fit to receive whatsoever by public authority shall be imprinted in them" (Hobbes [1651] 1968, chap. 30, 221). It is the new sovereign who must tell the people what they are to think, but since there is no longer any truth apart from the ruler's speech, this speech can no longer take on the personal and moral tones of the word "dissimulation." The sovereign of *Leviathan* is protected from any moral evaluation. In the *Discourses* Hobbes, in a sense, is more daring; here the moral language is not excluded but faced head-on, and Hobbes is willing to assert the unfashionable claim that the new prince must dissimulate in order to acquire power and, more important, secure it over time.

In a passage that well captures Hobbes's movement towards a world devoid of the traditional moral limits on political rule, he comments on Augustus' execution of war, beginning with claims concerning the just war, namely, that wars are just only if they are undertaken in defense of our lives, right, or honor; and he mocks those who set the "Law of State before the Law of God" (301–2). But in looking at the particular war against the Germans, an aggressive war with no injury to justify retribution, Hobbes concludes: "For oftentimes Kingdoms are better strengthened and defended by military reputation, than they are by the power of their Armies" (302). Despite the pieties noted a few lines above, the real issue is the preservation of the empire, not justice. And, just to be sure we recognize that, Hobbes adds almost as an afterthought: "And besides this, Augustus might find commodity in this war, by employing therein the great and active spirits, which else might have made themselves work at home, to the prejudice of his authority" (303). In a similar vein, towards the end of the discourse he recognizes how men "commonly measure their own virtues, rather by the acceptance that their persons find in the world, than by the judgment which their own conscience makes of them" (318–19). What establishes a reputation is "as often vicious as virtuous. For there is almost no civil action, but may proceed as well from evil as from good" (319).

Much of the first book of Tacitus' *Annales* addresses the problem of succession. Augustus, having established himself as the prince of the new regime, must identify the person who is to follow him in control of the state. The story Tacitus tells is of a founding prince who identifies a series of successors only to lose each one to an untimely death (287–95). Finally, Augustus is left with his less than pleasing stepson Tiberius. The problem of princely succession confronts Hobbes here. He has identified the principles of political foundings and pointed to the skills of one prince as the source of that founding against a disordered natural world. But individual skills alone are unable to sustain a regime beyond the time of the prince's death—or even the anticipation of death, for "when he dies, they are of necessity to begin again, and lay their foundation anew in the next" (310). The key development in Hobbes's political thought will be the generalization to a multitude of actors of the principles that he articulates here with reference to an individual. For Machiavelli this multitude becomes the basis for his republican theories as they appear in his own *Discourses,* a republic that he saw thriving on the conflict and disorder that inhered in regimes that prized their liberty. For Hobbes, the multitude did not lead to a theory of republicanism but to the search for a surer support for political order where one does not need to depend on the skills of one man to exercise *virtù;* where, in the language of the Dedicatory Epistle to *Leviathan,* all that was necessary was that the sovereign be there, like the geese on the Capitol who saved the Romans "not because they were they, but there."

The study of Augustus, the founder of the Principate, as sketched by Tacitus, shows how political foundings may come from the exercise of skills outside the traditional standards of moral behavior, but the history that follows and that Hobbes ignores in these early reflections identifies the problems of permanence for a regime so founded. Hobbes must progress beyond the model of the new prince embodied by Augustus to a regime founded on the basic power of all to recognize the need for order and to exercise the crafts or employ the intellectual efforts necessary to establish that order on their own.

The history that Tacitus records shows the wisdom of Augustus' efforts to identify a successor to prevent civil discord and to kill "the seeds of ambitious and traitorous hopes in those that think of alteration" (274). But identifying a successor cannot replace the security ensured by the establishment of principles or rules of authority that transcend the individual. The degeneration of the Roman Principate described in such vivid detail in Tacitus' writings demonstrates that the regime founded by the most politic of princes cannot last. As it turned out, that regime depended on the skill of one man; Hobbes's later writings acknowledge that the challenge of political order must go beyond the efforts of the one man skilled in the political crafts to include all members of the community, or as he puts it in *Leviathan,* men as the makers as well as the matter of the commonwealth.

After Hobbes wrote this discourse, he continued to use history as the basis for his political speculations and political exhortations at least through his decision to publish the translation of Thucydides in 1627, finally contenting himself that it would be of interest to the "few and better sort of readers" (Hobbes 1975, 9). In his autobiography he writes that he was an enthusiastic reader of ancient and modern history during the period when he composed the *Discourses* (*LW* 2:lxxxviii). As Machiavelli recognized, though, the study of the polities of the ancient world gives us insights into human behavior before the religious and moral impact of Christianity transformed the expectations of political leaders and rulers; it offers insights into foundings and institutions where issues of Christian doctrine can be set aside. But already Hobbes recognizes the limits that must attend the study of history itself as a guide to political understanding and action. It is limited, in particular, by the interests of the historian. Though Tacitus, in the famous phrase, claims to write his history *sine ira, sine studio* (without spleen, without partiality), most historians do not present the whole story or provide accurate lessons from which one can learn, but offer partial accounts driven by flattery or slander. Given men's passions, histories may obscure rather than illuminate the real causes of events. The sciences to which Hobbes later attaches himself escape the private passions of any particular story or storyteller. Histories ultimately turn out to be unreliable since "most men measuring others by themselves, are apt to think that all men will not only in this, but in all their actions more respect what conduces to the advancing of their own ends, than of truth, and the good of others" (249). The sciences appear to escape this problem; and as Hobbes comes to perceive it, the vanities of authors are not caught up in the stories that scientists tell. Discovering the sciences of geometry and physics, Hobbes finds a world where writers appear to work *sine ira, sine studio*. He thus discovers a new source in his search for historical maxims that will lead to order and protection from "the worst evil that can befall a State" (239).

History, so dependent on the personal passions of the storyteller, is likewise limited by its focus on the particular, the particular prince, the particular regime. Geometry as the deductive science which Hobbes discovered by chance on a trip to Europe in the early 1630s,[18] provides Hobbes with an escape from the particularity of history and suggests a way to generalize and equalize. In so doing, however, geometry and the other sciences to which Hobbes turns do not change the questions that he asks and the critical assumptions that lie at the core of those questions. Geometry allows for a universalized response to the problem of political foundings by generalizing to all the qualities attributed to the single founder. As the principles of political foundation are generalized, it will be the efforts of all, through authorization, that accomplish the transformation

18   If we are to believe Aubrey (1898 1:332).

from chaos to order. It will not be the one leader who manipulates but all those who have learned from Hobbes the true, original source of political order. Nevertheless, the science of geometry does not change the problem that Hobbes (and Machiavelli) had put at the center of the study of modern politics: how order emerges from chaos or how regimes can be instituted on the ashes of political conflict. "A Discourse upon the Beginning of Tacitus" shows us what his original questions and assumptions were—and why he saw the answers as insufficiently grounded.

A DISCOURSE OF ROME

Significantly, Hobbes studies political foundations in the first discourse through a careful sentence-by-sentence commentary on a historical text from pagan antiquity. In the second of the discourses published in the volume of the *Horae Subsecivae* Hobbes takes us to Rome. He had visited the Continent as tutor to William Cavendish, a trip that apparently included numerous nations and cities, but we have only his reflections on Rome, a city which as he phrases it had survived "a diversity of governments" (325).

Though much of the discourse purports to be about Roman sites, the introductory remarks make clear that once again it is political foundations that intrigue Hobbes, while the title reminds us of another discourse of Rome, that by Machiavelli on the founding of Rome as reported in the first ten books of Livy. An audience for secular travel literature in English appears to have developed in the first decades of the seventeenth century. In part, this literature on Italy and Europe in general may have been a response to the desire for descriptions of the voyages of discovery (Haynes 1986, 27). A number of weighty volumes were published about the time that Hobbes would have been writing this discourse on Rome (Coryat 1611, Sandys 1615, and Moryson 1617).[19] Most of these works con-

19 Moryson refers in his introduction to his "Discourses of severall commonwealths," but none of the authors of this travel literature uses the term "discourse" in the title of his book.

tained long descriptions of journeys, inns and food, of customs and folktales, of ruins and castles—or as one author says about Coryat, "half travel-diary, half guidebook" (Sells 1964). The publisher's note to Coryat's 1611 edition of his work comments: "On his return he proposed to publish his book of travels, but finding it difficult to induce any bookseller to undertake its publication, he applied to many eminent men to write 'panegyricke verses upon the Authour and his booke'" (1611, ix). The "panegyrickes" fill a fair number of pages and ensured publication of this particular travel book.[20]

Hobbes's discourse describing Rome is one of the earliest pieces reporting on an Englishman's travel to Rome.[21] His fascination with Rome comes, he claims, in part from the "divine power" (325) it had in antiquity, when Rome became "so great an empire" and its subsequent transformation through the Donation of Constantine into an empire of the popes. In that donation, Hobbes finds the "true Original" (327) of the dominion of the popes, a greatness claiming "supremacy in all causes, through all Kingdoms in the world" that has "more risen by encroachment than right" (328–29). In the previous discourse Hobbes had reflected on and learned from the establishment of political power by a politic prince. In this discourse, he eschews speculation on the source of political power except to suggest that perhaps it was the "fate of this place, that has ever been, or aimed to be the Mistress of the world" (329). What begins as a travelogue and continues in that fashion, nevertheless keeps reverting to issues of political power and its foundations. The study of the religious center of the Catholic world continues the study of political foundings, albeit of a very different sort.

Thus, a brief note on the harshness of the land turns into a disquisition on the effects of such a terrain on the morals and character of a people. More particularly, though, Hobbes

20 See Parr (1992) for a full discussion of Coryat and the emergence of the travelogue/guidebook in English literature.
21 As Hobbes suggests in his discourse (408–17), travel to Rome was seen as not without its dangers for a Protestant Englishman. Others traveling in Italy at this time describe attempts to disguise themselves so as not to be thought infidels. See especially Stoye (1952, 110–12, 119–22).

reflects on how the ease and comfort afforded by pleasant surroundings lead to a stagnancy of effort on behalf of one's
country and a lethargy that precipitates the loss of autonomy.
By nature, he tells us, men are "prone to an active life"; it is
"custom" that brings on the lethargy and the effeminacy that
make men subjects where they ought to rule (333). The language again recalls that of Machiavelli, who, at the beginning
of his own discourses, reflects on the impact of Rome's topography on the moral qualities of the early Romans. The observation that the luxury of a fertile land leads to servile popula-
tions is not unusual, but Hobbes's emphasis is not on morality
or the lack of it, but on action as natural and inaction as unnatural; he is concerned with the life of public energy rather than
with private affairs.

This section of the discourse shows that Hobbes still accepts the traditional models which extolled the worth of public
service and the honors that accrue to the one who serves his
state. The aristocratic pursuit of honor and glory tugs hard at
his understanding here, as when he criticizes the "easeful life"
which will dull the mind and lead a man to "grow retired,
applying himself to his own contents" (335–36). For such
men, "memory dies with them." And then Hobbes adds language that will startle any reader who interprets *Leviathan* as a
primer of egoism: "for no man is born only for himself" (336).
Hobbes here contrasts public service for the public good,
which brings honor, with what will later be called the bour-
geois value of private ends, which brings comforts to the individual without special regard for or impact on the public welfare. The hard life produces the former, the energy to act on
behalf of the welfare of the whole; the "easeful" life brings the
latter, the focus on the self which brings no honor.

The contrast as Hobbes presents it, though, has its own
complexities, especially if we refer back to the beginning of
Machiavelli's own *Discourses* and if we look forward to Hobbes's
later writings. In Hobbes's "Discourse of Rome," he notes that
ease and comfort have reduced men to a complacency that
makes them subject to the encroachments of others; harshness
would encourage an energy for public service. According to
Machiavelli, the fertility of the land and the serenity of the climate can reduce a people to complacency and consequently

subjection. But more significantly, Christianity, not the topography and the climate, offered the Italians peace in the future and a comfort that did not depend on the world at hand, leading them to ignore the oppression and enslavement that they were suffering. Machiavelli reminds the Italians that they have lost their freedom, that their complacency has made them slaves. The comfortable topography of their lives coming from Christian doctrine has withered the energy they need to save themselves. Machiavelli's self-imposed task is to make the Italians uncomfortable. Similarly in Hobbes's later writings the state of nature is designed to point readers to the discomforts which religion may hide, to the conditions from which they must protect themselves through the creation of civil society. He is in effect admonishing the English that, though they may live in the comfort of a stable government, they must remember the suffering, the harshness that lurks behind that comfort lest they allow themselves to be reduced to the brutishness of the natural condition of mankind or to the turmoil of civil war, the worst evil a state can experience.

One way to read Hobbes's mature political theory is to think of it as encouraging all to engage in an intellectual exercise that reminds us of what we have too casually forgotten: the nasty and brutish natural condition of mankind is like the harsh topography around Rome, an incentive to action, an incentive to the ambition to ameliorate the discomfort through political foundings. Ease may lead us to forget the necessity for political authority just as those whose wealth and luxury appear to come to them by nature, without effort, become enervated and unable to defend their possessions. The former will soon lose the ease and find themselves back in the natural condition; the latter will soon find their luxuries stolen by those with the energy to acquire. In the "Discourse of Rome" we see an early indication of the thought experiment Hobbes will later urge on his readers.

In these early writings, the honor attendant on public service still underlies Hobbes's vision of one's proper relationship to the political realm. In his later writings the individual concern with honor and glory is identified as destructive of political order rather than a prod to beneficial actions. Again, perhaps, we can see the equalizing effects of a science which he

discovers more than a decade later and which led him to aban-
don distinctions between degrees of birth. All—not just those
nobly motivated—must experience the ambition that leads
them to transform the harsh into the pleasant, the state of nature into civil society. In his early writings Hobbes can still extol
the notion of honorable public service that brings "memory"
or glory to an individual; later that honor inheres not in the
actions of any individual, but is ascribed to individuals by the
sovereign. On the other hand, the glory of creation belongs to
all who in their equal assertion against a harsh nature become
the creators of the leviathan; the task belongs not just to those
nobly inspired by the hope of eternal fame.

Following a catalogue of the numerous statues and monuments he observed throughout Rome, Hobbes reflects again
on glory and reputation, revealing his early belief that noble
action derives from promises of renown. He marvels that the
statues show a people more enthralled with virtue than with
greatness and concludes that the expectation of continued
fame among men "produced better effects of virtue and valor,
than Religion, and all other respects do in our days" (356).
The concern with reputation appears here a potent incentive
to noble action. But it is an incentive which will be rejected by
the later Hobbes, who will find in such a concern the denial
of the equality that must lie at the heart of the founding of
the state. That a desire to be first and foremost, whether in
reputation or in anything else, is destructive of the state must
be pointed out to Hobbes's later readers. Here, still under the
spell of aristocratic notions of public service and Machiavellian
visions of glory, Hobbes extols what he later condemns.[22]

Yet, the feisty, contrary Hobbes emerges in this essay as
well—the Hobbes who mocks common, self-satisfied opinions
and prejudices. He derides those who ridicule these monuments built in recognition of noble deeds. They scorn the ancients who, lacking any higher notion of eternal life, depend

---

22 This discourse especially offers support for Strauss's (1936) central thesis
concerning the aristocratic origins of Hobbes's moral theory and gives weight
to Thomas's (1965) effective garnering of passages from Hobbes's texts that
clearly demonstrate his ties and debts to the intellectual life and social mores
of the aristocrats among whom he lived.

on such monuments for their immortality. Hobbes defends the ancients, who "had some sense of the immortality of the soul" (361), though they were "only learned in natural sciences, and had no inspiration from above" (361–62); in turn, he scorns those of his contemporaries who in their "strange blindness . . . have such a mist before their eyes . . . that they will still turn the image of the incorruptible God, into the likeness of a corruptible man, which in any natural understanding, seems foolish" (363).

In the middle of the discourse, Hobbes's catalogue of sites again turns to broad reflections, this time on human credulity. While we should expect anti-popish pronouncements from an Englishman of Hobbes's religious upbringing, the peculiar focus of these pronouncements should intrigue us, as they are directed specifically to epistemological questions. He expresses alarm at the ease with which men are controlled by "shadows to conclude truth" (375) and how easily men are blinded by form and deceived into believing impossibilities as they give credence to miracles. These reflections come from Hobbes's observations upon religious antiquities and the relics in Rome, but also from "the gloriousness of their Altars, infinite numbers of images, priestly ornaments, and the divers actions they use in that service; besides the most excellent and exquisite Music of the world, that surprises our ears" (389–90). The Church having access to such wondrous displays is able "to catch men's affections, and to ravish their understanding" (389) and by repeating tales of miracles—even those which are proved false—churchmen "delude the people" (391). At one point Hobbes suggests, "A man might spin out a long discourse of such a subject" (377–78). Indeed, he later does so when he begins *Leviathan* with "concerning the thoughts of men," and when he concludes that lengthy book with a detailed section on the Kingdom of Darkness. In this discourse the "miracle of the two chains" (373–74) leads to his awe at human credulity. It is just this credulity that leads to the instability of polities; it is this credulity that must be replaced with the firm epistemological foundations of Hobbes's empiricism.

Hobbes's tone when describing the Roman's belief in miraculous causes and the attribution of such miracles to some saint or another is scornful, but even when mocking men's credulity Hobbes never loses sight of his search for causes. He sees the Romans, attempting to understand their world and the proximate causes for the events in it, accepting the Church's explanation of saints and direct divine intervention into their daily activities. Such credulity precludes efforts at true understanding and remains unsatisfactory, worthy of ridicule. The search for causes, though, so unsatisfactorily practiced in the Rome of the popes, does dominate Hobbes's thought as he later turns to science for causes independent of any divine intervention.

While Hobbes's travelogue illustrates the epistemological turn to his intellect, and while his observations illuminate the religious role of Rome as devoted to the salvation of the human soul, he also analyses the city of Rome as a purely political institution. He asks of the city political questions: can it protect itself from invasion, what sort of "government" does it have, how wealthy is it? (395–96). The answers to these questions in turn lead to reflections on how similar the Church is in its actions to the temporal princes. With its ambassadors and its goings and comings, with its outward aspects of honor, it is "behind none" of the "greatest Princes" of the world (398). The temporal ambitions and pride of the popes and of the cardinals bring Hobbes to a critique of Rome on political grounds. The pope and his cardinals are proud and ambitious, like the ambitious man writ large, the one Hobbes warned us about in the "Discourse upon the Beginning of Tacitus" who is a danger to any honest man that stands behind him or before him, destroying the former out of fear, the latter out of hope (300). Such men become the teachers, by example, of what they oppose by precept, educating their followers to "ambitious thoughts, and unsatisfied desires after the wealth and glory of this world" (404). The ambitions of the Church become more than a simple political hazard in the relations between nations. By its own example the Church educates people in just those vices that are destructive of civil order, just those qualities of character against which the Hobbesian laws of nature advise (*Leviathan,* chap. 15). The attack on the Roman Church goes well beyond doctrine; indeed, apart from the discussion of miracles, little is included in this discourse about doctrine. It is rather the politics of Rome that intrigues Hobbes and gives this discourse its place in his early political thought.

A DISCOURSE OF LAWS

In his "Discourse upon the Beginning of Tacitus," Hobbes searches for the sources of political order in the personal actions of a new prince in a new state. He points to the policy of a prince who can "extinguish" his former allies and can lure his subjects to obedience with the "vacancy of war" and with grain for their tables. In the midst of the discussion of the harsh and sometimes duplicitous measures that Augustus took in order to assure order in the newly founded state, Hobbes refers to the laws in effect at the time of the Roman Republic. They are like "Spiders' webs, only to hold the smaller Flies" (272) and cannot function to restrain the strong or to ensure the stability that a new prince can provide. When Augustus took power he had to put his "authority" behind the preexisting laws so that they would no longer be so easily disregarded. Laws in the discourse on Tacitus, then, appear as part of the tool kit of the new prince. In his "Discourse of Laws," Hobbes appears to be considerably more sanguine about the potential that laws may have to structure society and protect a political order in which men live peaceful and secure lives. In a sense, the laws here replace the prince from the discourse on Tacitus.[23] They are the "Princes we ought to serve, the Captains we are to follow" (506).

Despite its optimistic view of what laws can accomplish, the discourse on laws makes evident what life without laws would be like and so demonstrates why we need political authority and political restraints, why "by the fear, and terror of them, men's audacities might be repressed" (507). Hobbes offers us

23 The word "replace" may suggest a chronological order to the essays. We cannot make such a claim and cannot know in which order the discourses published in this volume were composed. It may be that the discourse on Tacitus is a later work and as such moves directly into the theoretical principles at the basis of Hobbes's thought, and that the "Discourse of Laws" shows Hobbes's early explorations where laws still seem more than "spiders' webs" and have the potential to bring order to disorder.

an early adumbration of what he will later call the natural condition of mankind. In the discourse on Tacitus we have allusions to civil wars that plagued the Romans under the Republic. In the discourse on laws we find a more general statement of that condition. Hobbes uses words like "confusion" (507, 514), "convulsion," and "dissolution" (516), and phrases such as "an overthrow to conversation, and commerce amongst men" and "all right would be perverted by power, and all honesty swayed by greatness" (507) to describe a world in which men are not restrained by the rule of law. Laws protect us from "all such violent and unlawful courses, as otherwise liberty would insinuate" (508). At one point he claims, "For where Laws be wanting, there neither Religion, nor Life, nor society can be maintained" (517), strongly suggesting religion's dependence on laws. But it is his warning that "a man had better choose to live where no thing than where all things be lawful" (516) that captures what will characterize his later presentation of the state of nature and our need to escape it.

Where all things are lawful, there men enjoy the rights to all things and there confusion and convulsion follow. There we can rightly ask: "who is it that can say, 'This is my House, or my Land, or my money, or my goods'?" (519). There men will measure their actions not "by the rule of *Aequum* and *Iustum*, but by the square of their own benefit, and affections" (508). Hobbes here performs the mental exercise that he urges us to do in his later political works when he asks us to imagine the state of nature—we are to imagine places where the laws do not restrain. To imagine such a place is to recognize that property does not exist by nature, that it depends on the voice of the lawmaker(s). To imagine such a place is to recognize that justice is not self-enforcing; self-interest is. Men not restrained by power act as "their own wills, and inclination would give them leave to effect" (508), to the detriment of a life of security, not to mention prosperity.

To claim, as Hobbes does frequently throughout this discourse, that without laws human society dissolves is hardly a novel argument. For support Hobbes can return to such classical authorities as Plato and Heraclitus; he can cite readily the relevant passages from their works (and he does, 509–10). But while the language that Hobbes uses to emphasize the chaos

resulting from the absence of justice and secure property fore-
shadows the language we find later in his treatment of political
society, the more significant aspect of these sections of the discourse is the suggestion that law acts in opposition to nature.[24]
For Plato and Heraclitus, and for medieval natural-law theory
as well, law is reason and reason derives from nature. There is
no opposition between that which is natural and that which
the laws command. For Hobbes there is—and there is not. In
other words, the "Discourse of Laws" suggests that Hobbes has
not yet resolved the relationship among law and reason and
nature as he will in his later writings. The resolution that he
offers later with his presentation of the various laws of nature
is among the most radical of his redefinitions of traditional
language, but here in his early work we see him still struggling
with an opposition between a nature that provides no natural
grounds for property or justice and a nature that gives us the
reason to discover laws.

On the one hand, Hobbes argues that "we receive much
more benefit from Laws in this kind [those that bridle the
claims of others], than from Nature" (520). On the other
hand, he accepts the language of traditional natural-law theory
whereby our laws derive from our reason which derives from
nature. Hobbes tells us in this discourse that by nature men
are affected "with a violent heat of desires, and passions and
fancies"; by "natural inclination" men are prone to "all manner
of hazards and ill" (520). These are the natural inclinations
and passions that the laws created or "invented" (522) by men
and applied by human officers must restrain. The opposition
is between nature and human art. Order is not inherent in the
natural world; it is imposed by human effort and human reason. In the discourse describing the rise of Augustus it was the
individual policy of the prince that could impose order on the
disorder left by the conflicts of civil war; in this discourse, a
quieter and tamer work, Hobbes focuses on laws as the mecha-

24 Bobbio (1993, 36) writing about Hobbes's later thought phrases it this
way: "Artifice no longer imitates nature, but is equal to it. This change is a sign
that things made by human beings, and human industry in general, are now
seen in a new light and valued more highly." This insight is appropriate to the
Discourses as well.

nism for human restraint; laws once created and written by humans can outlast their authors but still impose an order that is contrary to nature. To capture the thrust of these early writings, we must attend to the way in which he establishes the imposition of order on a disordered universe as the central human challenge. Augustus illustrates one way; laws as human exercises in control over "confusion" and "convulsion" illustrate another.

The complexity emerges, however, when Hobbes draws into his discourse on laws the language of natural-law theory that unites law with nature in a way that contradicts his earlier portrait of a naturally disordered world. In a section that could almost come from St. Thomas Aquinas, Hobbes discusses the law of nature which is "common to every living creature, and not only incident to Men: as for example, the commixture of several sexes . . ." (518). He discusses the "fountains of natural Justice" from which the infinite variety of laws derive (524–25) and describes the unity of law and reason (531).[25] Whereas elsewhere he will combine law and reason, in this discourse he, on occasion, unites law and nature.

While this embrace of natural law may be disconcerting for those eager to find in these discourses the Hobbes known as the critic of defenders of common law such as Coke and the precursor of positive-law theory, we do, nevertheless, find in the elaboration of this point the direction in which Hobbes will move. After his assertion of natural law along scholastic lines, Hobbes quickly turns to civil and municipal law. These are the laws over which his attention lingers as he speaks of the origins of Roman law (i.e., pre-Christian law); he reiterates that it is law—now municipal law—that defines property, the mine and thine of civil society. The ties of generation, for in-

---

25 The laws of nature that will figure in Hobbes's later works on politics are likewise related to reason, as deductions of reason (e.g., *Leviathan,* esp. chaps. 14 and 15), but the definition of reason has changed radically from that used for natural-law theory of the medieval period. It is in Hobbes's appropriation of the terms "reason" and "law of nature" that we might identify his inversion of traditional thought rather than his continuation of it. See Bobbio (1993, 118); but also Fuller (1990), who suggests affinities between St. Thomas Aquinas and Hobbes in terms of their understandings of the relation of law to reason.

stance, are inadequate to ensure the passing of wealth from parent to child. "Whatsoever is left unto us by Testament of another, it is impossible we should ever keep it as our own, if Law restrained not others' claims, and confirmed them not unto us" (519–20). Nature by itself accounts for nothing; the natural desire to leave what is ours to our descendants is not self-enforcing. Only the laws which depend on the "dispensers and interpreters" (521) for their existence and enforcement can ensure the satisfaction of our natural desires.

A section of the discourse that analyzes the spur to making laws—be it fear or reason—is followed by a section that describes the infinite variety of laws that derive from the fountains of natural justice (524–25). Here the civil law attached to the particularities of place and time comes not from the authority of the prince, the speech of Augustus, for example, but from those fountains of natural justice. Differences in laws in different states arise not because of the authority of different speakers but because the landscape through which the waters from the fountain of natural justice run will differ from place to place, giving a different taste to the laws of each state. The metaphor is purple and forced, and the consistency of argument so characteristic of the later Hobbes is missing.

Before Hobbes can reach the classic Hobbesian understanding of natural law and of the place of law within the political community, he will need to shed a natural-law theory that posits a natural and perceptible justice from which civil laws derive. The tension in the "Discourse of Laws" partly arises from a mind still accepting a natural-law theory as articulated in the medieval period but recognizing that law is constructed by humans to restrain nature in order to build an unnatural order. There is no evidence here of the magical transformation Hobbes will later perform when he unites law and nature to describe the exercise of human reason discovering the principles of self-preservation. Here he still writes about the fountains of natural justice and, for the moment, with quotes from Cicero, defines law as reason applied to the particularities of the situation (531).

The common source of law in reason does confront Hobbes with the difficulty of explaining the varieties of laws. This is easy whether he uses the fountain and stream image noted above or when he makes reference to different intentions of the "first Planters" (533) of polities. But this challenge does lead Hobbes to address the precise origins of these diverse laws, and he proposes to use ancient Rome as an example, offering a typology of the variety of sources for that state's laws, from those ordained by the power of the Senate (the *senatus consultum*) to those given as "commandments of the General in the Field" (536–38). The typology of Roman law makes explicit the origin of law in speech. In this discussion he has left behind the question of the specific law's relation to the fountain of natural justice and its dependence on the local landscape. That which pleases the prince, *principium placita,* goes along with laws propounded by the people as a *plebiscitum.*

As if to confound us, however, Hobbes turns this discussion of Roman law to a consideration of the unwritten laws or customs which arise over time and which have no "known Author" (541).[26] To these he grants the same power and authority as those laws which come from the official actions of the political units. The discourse ends, then, with a discomforting equation of common law based on custom with law that is based on civil statutes. Hobbes's embrace of both forms of law, giving each full authority and legitimacy, will slacken as his thought matures. He will recognize the threat to political obedience and political obligation that emerges from allowing the validity of common law (Herzog 1989, 137). Indeed, custom and common law will disappear from his model, and statutes whose "author" is "known" will be the only way to ensure that the "confusions" and "convulsions" that laws prevent do not destroy the security and prosperity that men seek. The contradictions that Hobbes poses in this discourse will be resolved as he clarifies his own analyses of political origins and institutions. But these contradictions show what challenges must be met in the movement from the medieval worldview to the

---

26   As Cropsey (1971, 11) notes, Hobbes does not become involved in a controversy with Coke over the position of common law during Coke's tenure as chief justice. The explicit rejection of Coke's views comes in *Leviathan* and in *A Dialogue between a Philosopher and a Student of the Common Laws of England,* probably written well after the completion of *Leviathan* (Cropsey 1971, 3).

deeply rationalistic foundations of Hobbes's later political thought, as well as of liberal thought in general.

These early writings by Hobbes leave us with the question of how his ideas developed as the result of his subsequent encounters with other intellectual traditions, in particular the scientific concerns of his contemporaries in England and on the Continent. The *Discourses* help us to structure that question. What we have here is Hobbes's thought unaffected by scientific models; it thus puts us in a position to evaluate how the scientific method altered (or did not alter) the issues Hobbes raised and the answers he provided. The answer to this question should lead us to a deeper understanding of the basis of modern political thought. I would suggest that the questions at the core of his thought are vividly present in these prescientific writings; Hobbes's later search was primarily for a method appropriate to address these issues. In science he found the abstraction from and the absence of *ira* and *studium* that created difficulties with historical sources of knowledge. But this new epistemological base does not mean the abandonment of the puzzle he defines early in his writings—the puzzle of the sources of political order. What he gains is new insight into how the modern world might address this puzzle; what he began with was a recognition of the challenges the modern world faced.

Part Four

Statistical Wordprinting

STATISTICAL WORDPRINTING

Noel B. Reynolds

S TATISTICAL WORDPRINTING arose in the second half of this century as scholars searched for scientific means of establishing the authorship of contested texts, much in the way criminal investigators use fingerprinting. Wordprinting is still in its infancy and cannot yet boast an explanatory theory or even a single agreed-upon name. Nor do its practitioners agree on an optimal statistical model. This degree of openness in wordprinting has not prevented the convincing success of a number of important studies, which success in turn gives added intuitive plausibility to its basic assumption. That assumption is that under normal circumstances any individual's writings will be consistent between themselves in the relative frequency of specific noncontextual-word patterns[1] used, but that writings from different authors will exhibit significantly different relative frequencies for these noncontextual-word patterns. In psycholinguistic terms this amounts to the claim that as individuals learn and master a language, they subconsciously develop permanent habits of patterned noncontextual-word usage. Because these patterns are mostly subconscious, they are not usually subject to intentional or even accidental modification, even when an author shifts genres or attempts to imitate someone else. And to the extent that wordprinting tests focus on noncontextual-word patterns, the mea-

---

1 See note 16 in Part 1 above

surements they produce tend not to vary much with variations of textual content.

The availability of computers to scholars in the humanities has allowed for extensive use of wordprinting. Entering the texts themselves into the computer makes it possible to analyze larger texts and to check them for large numbers of identifying word patterns. The results of this counting can then be analyzed through statistical comparisons. The Hobbes study alone produced over 2,100 separate statistical tests measuring 65 different word patterns each. Clearly, this would have been an impossible task before the arrival of computers.

While there are many wordprinting models available, we chose to avoid some of the more powerful but unverified techniques, and turned instead to the conservative and laborious wordprinting model developed by John L. Hilton and his early Berkeley associates,[2] engaging Hilton himself as a collaborator in the Hobbes study. Various dimensions of Hilton's development of the Berkeley group's statistical model are described below. As will be shown, this technique avoids assumptions of normal distribution, controls the noise (statistical effects of irrelevant information) introduced in the process of text selection and excerpting, uses statistical benchmark measures established through extensive testing in control-author studies, and pre-tests each proposed text to be sure it is typical of unconstrained single-author writing before applying wordprint analyses to it. These distinctive features of Hilton's technique avoid the inherent risks of subjective appeals to intuition that characterize most other approaches, as well as unwarranted assumptions about the distribution of identifying word patterns. The potential drawback to Hilton's approach is that its conservatism will not allow clear determinations of authorship in all cases but predicts ambiguity in about 30 percent of all comparisons. Fortunately, the differences and similarities found in our analyses of Hobbes and the *Horae Subsecivae* were sufficiently clear to avoid ambiguity.

Since moving to Brigham Young University, Hilton has

2   See Hilton (1990, 94–95) for an account of the Berkeley group and its contributions to this model. Hilton and Jenkins (1987) report the group's work.

modified and extended the model that he first developed with Jenkins and others in the 1980s (Hilton 1995).[3] The first step is to select texts for comparison and identify word blocks of 4,998 words each. In the Hobbes study we divided the *Horae Subsecivae* into ten of these blocks and selected for comparison 17 blocks from Hobbes's known writings, eight from Francis Bacon, and six from Fulke Greville. These text blocks were then coded as necessary to enable the computer to count the occurrences of noncontextual-word patterns as described below.

In an attempt to establish continuity with other leading wordprinting endeavors, Hilton chose to use a set of 65 non-contextual-word-pattern ratios proposed by A. Q. Morton (1978).[4] The problems that have been noted in Morton's model are avoided in Hilton's use of these 65 patterns.[5] The 65 measures, which are calculated for each word block, are listed in the Appendix.

Once these measures are tabulated for each 4,998-word text block, a nonparametric[6] null-hypothesis statistical test is calculated for each of the 65 measures in comparisons between all of the blocks. The numerical sum of these statistically significant null-hypothesis rejections is then calculated for each block, relative to every other block in the study. When

3   A working paper describing the earlier model was widely distributed (Hilton and Jenkins 1987). It can be obtained from F.A.R.M.S., 315 AKH, Brigham Young University, Provo, Utah 84602. The interest of Brigham Young University statisticians in wordprinting focused originally on studies of Book of Mormon authorship (Larsen and Rencher [1980] and Hilton [1990]).

4   See Appendix Three for a listing of all 65 word patterns used in the Hobbes study. While it is clear that not all of these are effective discriminators of authorship for the texts in our study, we have retained the entire set to maintain continuity between the Hobbes study and the earlier control-author studies that established our basic measures of statistical significance.

5   See M. W. A. Smith (1985a,b).

6   Nonparametric tests such as the Mann-Whitney statistic have been developed for use with data which can only give weak conclusions using standard parametric tests such as chi-square, Student "t," or regular multivariate analysis of variance. Parametric tests assume the data are normally distributed (producing a bell-shaped curve) and that sample sizes are large. Where these assumptions are not met, more powerful results can be obtained by the use of nonparametric tests.

these sums are too high (according to the benchmark measures), we conclude that the two texts being compared probably do not have the same author.

In control studies on known authors, Hilton established statistically significant ranges for distinguishing texts by different authors. Comparisons between texts by the same author almost never yield more than six null-hypothesis rejections and measure a gross mean of 2.58 rejections. Texts by different authors tend to produce many more rejections and measure a gross mean of 8.26. When seven rejections are used as a cutoff, 70 percent of the between-author comparisons clearly distinguish text blocks as probably having separate authors, while 30 percent remain ambiguous. The histograms in Part 1 of this study show the text blocks drawn from the larger half of the *Horae Subsecivae* to be unambiguously outside the range of same-author works when compared with Hobbes's known writings. Similarly, text blocks drawn from the three *Horae* discourses published in this volume were also unambiguously within the range of same-author works when compared with Hobbes's known writings. Had the test results for these three discourses fallen in the ambiguous range, we could not so confidently assign them to Hobbes.

The basic wordprint technique described above has several additional features that Hilton and the Berkeley group developed to eliminate noise, to increase statistical reliability, and to identify texts that are unsuitable for wordprint analysis. To avoid assuming normal distributions of statistical null-hypothesis rejections, they used the Mann-Whitney nonparametric statistic ($p < .05$). This approach increased author discrimination by unambiguously identifying 50 percent more of the paired control-texts written by different authors than was possible with the traditional chi-square statistic.

After considerable experimentation, the Berkeley group was able to optimize word-block size. Optimization is a compromise between using word blocks so small that reliable statistics are unattainable and blocks so large that significant but shorter texts cannot be analyzed. They achieved clearest results with 4,998-word blocks subdivided into 17 smaller blocks of 294 words each. Each of the 65 Morton measures which occurs five or more times is calculated for each of these blocks.

Each block is next compared with every other block for each of these measures (usually 40–45), and those that measure statistically different (null-hypothesis rejections) are summed for each comparison. At this point a large number (seven or more) of null-hypothesis rejections justifies concluding that the two blocks under consideration have different authors. In this Hobbes study none of the three *Horae Subsecivae* discourses ever produced over five null-hypothesis rejections in comparison with any of the known Hobbes texts.

To eliminate the noise introduced by the arbitrary beginning and ending points of the subdivisions for the 4,998-word blocks, the Berkeley group developed wraparound partitioning. Each 4,998-word block is divided into seventeen smaller blocks of 294 words for variance measurements. Each block's noncontextual word-patterns are counted seven times, starting 42 words further into the block each time and linking the end of the block to the beginning in wraparound fashion ($7 \times 42 \times 17 = 4,998$). Each of these seven countings is compared to each of the seven countings for each other block in the analysis. The median number of null-hypothesis rejections in each of these 49 comparisons is used as the measure of difference between the two texts being compared.

Not all texts are equally suitable for wordprint analysis. Texts which have been coauthored, heavily edited, or contain a lot of quotations or paraphrasing or texts written under constraints imposed by radical genre change or external circumstances are not as likely to reflect an author's normal wordprint. Hilton has formulated this as another form of noise, drawing on information theory, and has developed an experimental form of the Mood test to measure the ratio of signal (desired information) to noise (S/N). This test is used on all 4,998-word blocks to determine whether they are likely to be usable in wordprinting analysis. It was this test that demonstrated the problematic character of the Bacon texts we had wanted to use for one of our control sets for the Hobbes study.

Wordprinting or stylometric studies are becoming more frequent and more important throughout the humanities as scholars turn to statistical analyses of digitized texts for assistance in resolving issues of authorship. Yet, all work in this area remains to some degree experimental and unavoidably rests on some ad hoc theorizing and methodology, with many research design questions being governed mostly by intuition. The successes of such studies indicate an enormous future potential for scholarly work in the humanities. But the lack of a fully tested and universalized methodology seriously hampers progress in this area.

Appendix 1

Table of Contents of the 1620 Horae Subsecivae

TITLES (in order)		NUMBER OF PAGES
	OBSERVATIONS	
1	Of Arrogance	10
2	Of Ambition	20
3	Of Affectation	22
4	Of Detraction	22
5	Of Selfe-will	11
6	Of Masters and Servants	18
7	Of Expences	11
8	Of Visitations	10
9	Of Death	11
10	Of a Country Life	41
11	Of Religion	17
12	Of Reading History	30
	DISCOURSES	
1	Upon the Beginning of Tacitus	102
2	Of Rome	94
3	Against Flatterie	86
4	Of Lawes	37

APPENDIX 2

TEXTS AND WORD BLOCKS ANALYZED

HORAE SUBSECIVAE[1]

Blocks 1–2[2]	Of Arrogance
	Of Ambition
	Of Affectation
	Of Detraction
	Of Selfe-will
	Of Masters and Servants
	Of Expences
	Of Visitations
	Of Death
	Of Reading History
Block 3	Of a Country Life
	Of Religion (first 84 lines)
Blocks 4–5	A Discourse upon the Beginning of Tacitus
Block 6	A Discourse of Lawes
	Of Religion (lines 86–170)
Block 7	A Discourse Against Flatterie (lines 1–505)
Block 8	A Discourse Against Flatterie (last part)
	Of Religion (lines 171–185)
Blocks 9–10	A Discourse of Rome

---

1   This order of essays and discourses varies slightly from the text.
2   These texts are lumped in order and then divided in two.

THOMAS HOBBES

Block 1   On the Life and History of Thucydides
Blocks 2–7   *Leviathan*
Blocks 8–13   *On the Elements of Law*
Blocks 14–17   *Behemoth*

FRANCIS BACON

Block 1   *The Essayes or Counsels, Civill and Morall*[3]
         Of Honour and Reputation
         Of Expence
         Of Regiment of Health
         Of Discourse
         Of Negociating
         Of Followers and Frends
         Of Sutours
         Of Studies
         Of Faction
         Of Ceremonies and Respects
Block 2   Essays new in the 1612 or 1625 edition
         Of Truth
         Of Death
         Of Unity in Religion
         Of Revenge
         Of Adversity
         Of Simulation and Dissimulation
         Of Parents and Children
         Of Marriage and the Single Life
         Of Envy
         Of Love
         Of Great Place
         Of Boldness
         Of Goodness and Goodness of Nature
Blocks 3–4   *The Second Part of . . . The New Organon*
Blocks 5–8   *The Advancement of Learning*

FULKE GREVILLE

Blocks 1–6   *Prose Works of Fulke Greville, Lord Brooke*

---

3   Block 1 includes the 1626 edition of essays first published in 1597.

Appendix 3

The 65 noncontextual-word patterns developed by A. Q. Morton, and incorporated into the Hilton wordprinting instrument, are listed below.

1. The fraction of all sentences with "a" in which "a" is the first word of the sentence.

2. The fraction of all sentences with "an" in which "an" is the first word of the sentence.

3. The fraction of all sentences with "and" in which "and" is the first word of the sentence.

4. The fraction of all sentences with "in" in which "in" is the first word of the sentence.

5. The fraction of all sentences with "it" in which "it" is the first word of the sentence.

6. The fraction of all sentences with "it" in which "it" is the last word of the sentence.

7. The fraction of all sentences with "of" in which "of" is the first word of the sentence.

8. The fraction of all sentences with "of" in which "of" is the penultimate word of the sentence.

9. The fraction of all sentences with "the" in which "the" is the first word of the sentence.

10. The fraction of all sentences with "the" in which "the" is the penultimate word of the sentence.

11. The fraction of all sentences with "with" in which "with" is the penultimate word of the sentence.

12. The fraction of all occurrences of "a" in which "a" is the penultimate word of the sentence.

13. The fraction of all occurrences of "a" which precede an adjective.

14. The fraction of all occurrences of "a" in which "a" is followed by some other word plus "and."

15. The fraction of all occurrences of "a" in which "a" is followed by some other word plus "of."

16. The fraction of all occurrences of "a" in which "a" is followed by some other word plus "a" again.

17. The fraction of all occurrences of "a" in which "a" is followed by two other words plus "a" again.

18. The fraction of all occurrences of "and" in which "and" is followed by an adjective.

19. The fraction of all occurrences of "and" in which "and" is followed by "the."

20. The fraction of all occurrences of "and" in which "and" is followed by another word plus "of."

21. The fraction of all occurrences of "and" in which "and" is followed by another word plus "and" again.

22. The fraction of all occurrences of "and" in which "and" is followed by two other words plus "and" again.

23. The fraction of all occurrences of "as" in which "as" is followed by another word plus "as" again.

24. The fraction of all occurrences of "as" in which "as" is followed by two other words plus "as" again.

25. The fraction of all occurrences of "be" in which "be" is followed by "a."

26. The fraction of all occurrences of "be" in which "be" is preceded by "to."

27. The fraction of all occurrences of "but" in which "but" is followed by "a."

28. The fraction of all occurrences of "by" in which "by" is followed by "the."

29. The fraction of all occurrences of "I" in which "I" is followed by "am."

30. The fraction of all occurrences of "I" in which "I" is followed by "have."

31. The fraction of all occurrences of "I" in which "I" is followed by some other word plus "I" again.

32. The fraction of all occurrences of "I" in which "I" is followed by two other words plus "I" again.

33. The fraction of all occurrences of "in" in which "in" is followed by "a."

34. The fraction of all occurrences of "in" in which "in" is followed by "the."

35. The fraction of all occurrences of "of" in which "of" is followed by "a."

36. The fraction of all occurrences of "of" in which "of" is followed by "the."

37. The fraction of all occurrences of "of" in which "of" is followed by some other word plus "and."

38. The fraction of all occurrences of "the" in which "the" is preceded by "and."

39. The fraction of all occurrences of "the" in which "the" is preceded by "of."

40. The fraction of all occurrences of "the" in which "the" is preceded by "in."

41. The fraction of all occurrences of "the" in which "the" is preceded by "to."

42. The fraction of all occurrences of "the" in which "the" is followed by some other word plus "and."

43. The fraction of all occurrences of "the" in which "the" is followed by some other word plus "the" again.

44. The fraction of all occurrences of "the" in which "the" is followed by two other words plus "the" again.

45. The fraction of all occurrences of "to" in which "to" is followed by "be."

46. The fraction of all occurrences of "to" in which "to" is followed by "the."

47. The fraction of all occurrences of "to" in which "to" is followed by some other word plus "to" again.

48. The fraction of all occurrences of "to" in which "to" is followed by two other words plus "to" again.

49. The fraction of all occurrences of "you" in which "you" is followed by some other word plus "you" again.

50. The fraction of all occurrences of "you" in which "you" is followed by two other words plus "you" again.

51. The fraction of all occurrences of "to" which are located between two verbs.

52. The total occurrences of "an" divided by itself plus the total occurrences of "a."

53. The total occurrences of "any" divided by itself plus the total occurrences of "all."

54. The total occurrences of "no" divided by itself plus the total occurrences of "not."

55. The total occurrences of "up" divided by itself plus the total occurrences of "upon."

56. The total occurrences of "with" divided by itself plus the total occurrences of "without."

57. All occurrences of "a" preceding a word unique in the text block divided by all occurrences of "a" which both follow and precede words unique in the text block.

58. All occurrences of "and" preceding a word unique in the text block divided by all occurrences of "and" which both follow and precede words unique in the text block.

59. All occurrences of "in" preceding a word unique in the text block divided by all occurrences of "in" which both follow and precede words unique in the text block.

60. All occurrences of "it" preceding a word unique in the text block divided by all occurrences of "it" which both follow and precede words unique in the text block.

61. All occurrences of "I" preceding a word unique in the text block divided by all occurrences of "I" which both follow and precede words unique in the text block.

62. All occurrences of "of" preceding a word unique in the text block divided by all occurrences of "of" which both follow and precede words unique in the text block.

63. All occurrences of "that" preceding a word unique in the text block divided by all occurrences of "that" which both follow and precede words unique in the text block.

64. All occurrences of "the" preceding a word unique in the text block divided by all occurrences of "the" which both follow and precede words unique in the text block.

65. All occurrences of "to" preceding a word unique in the text block divided by all occurrences of "to" which both follow and precede words unique in the text block.

BIBLIOGRAPHY

Arber, Edward. 1875–77. *A Transcript of the Registers of the Company of London, 1554–1640 A.D.* 5 volumes. London: Privately printed.

Aubrey, John. 1898. *"Brief Lives," chiefly of Contemporaries, set down by John Aubrey, between the years of 1669 & 1696.* Edited from the author's manuscript by Andrew Clark. Oxford: At the Clarendon Press.

Beal, Peter. 1987. *English Literary Manuscripts.* London: Mansell.

Bickley, Francis. 1911. *The Cavendish Family.* London: Constable.

Bobbio, Norberto. 1993. *Thomas Hobbes and the Natural Law Tradition.* Translated by Daniela Gobetti. Chicago: University of Chicago Press.

Brydges, Sir S. E. 1802. *Memoirs of the Peers of England during the Reign of James the First.* London: Printed for J. White by Nichols.

Burke, Peter. 1969. "Tacitism." In *Tacitus,* edited by T. A. Dorey, 149–71. London: Routledge & Kegan Paul.

Bush, Douglas. 1945. *British Literature in the Earlier Seventeenth Century, 1600–1660.* Oxford: Oxford University Press.

Bush, Douglas. 1973. "Hobbes, William Cavendish, and 'Essayes'." *Notes and Queries.* New series, 20(May): 162–64.

Bywaters, David and Steven N. Zwicker. 1989. "Politics and Translation: The English Tacitus of 1698." *The Huntington Library Quarterly* 52: 319–46.

Coryat, Thomas. [1611] 1905. *Coryat's Crudities, hastily gobbled up in five Moneths travells in France, Savoy, Italy, Rhetia.* . . . Glasgow: James McLehose & Sons, Publishers to the University.

Cropsey, Joseph, ed. 1971. *Thomas Hobbes, "A Dialogue between a Philosopher and a Student of the Common Laws of England."* Chicago: University of Chicago Press.

Fuller, Timothy. 1990. "Compatibilities on the Idea of Law in Thomas Aquinas and Thomas Hobbes." *Hobbes Studies* 3:112–24.

Gabrieli, Vittorio. 1957. "Bacone, La Riforma e Roma Nella Versione Hobbesiana d'un Carteggio di Fulgenzio Micanzio." *English Miscellany* 8:195–250.

Gauthier, David. 1969. *The Logic of Leviathan: The Moral and Political Theory of Thomas Hobbes.* Oxford: Clarendon Press.

Goldsmith, M. M. 1966. *Hobbes's Science of Politics.* New York: Columbia University Press.

Greenleaf, W. H. 1964. *Order, Empiricism and Politics: Two Traditions of English Political Thought, 1500- 1700.* London: Oxford University Press.

Grove, Joseph. 1764. "The Life of William the Second Earl of Devonshire." *The Lives of All the Earls and Dukes of Devonshire.* London: Privately printed.

Hamilton, John Jay. 1978. "Hobbes's Study and the Hardwick Library." *Journal of the History of Philosophy* 16:445–53.

Hampton, Jean. 1986. *Hobbes and the Social Contract Tradition.* Cambridge: Cambridge University Press.

Harwood, John T. 1986. *The Rhetorics of Thomas Hobbes and Bernard Lamy.* Carbondale: Southern Illinois University Press.

Haynes, Jonathan. 1986. *The Humanist as Traveler: George Sandys's "Relation of a Journey begun An. Dom. 1610."* Rutherford: Fairleigh Dickinson University Press.

Herzog, Don. 1989. *Happy Slaves: A Critique of Consent Theory.* Chicago: University of Chicago Press.

Hiatt, Tim. 1993. "Can Authors Alter Their Wordprints? James Joyce's Ulysses." Master's thesis, Brigham Young University.

Hilton, John L. 1990. "On Verifying Wordprint Studies: Book of Mormon Authorship." *BYU Studies* 30 (Summer): 89–108.

Hilton, John L. 1995. "Development and Testing of Nonparametric Ergodic Procedures Usable for Objective Author Identification on 5000-Word Tests." *Journal of Literary and Linguistic Computing.* Forthcoming

Hilton, John L. and Kenneth D. Jenkins. 1987. "On Maximizing Author Identification by Measuring 5000-Word Blocks." *F.A.R.M.S.*

Papers. Provo, Utah: Foundation for Ancient Research and Mormon Studies.

Hobbes, Thomas. 1839–45. *Opera Philosophica Quae Latine Scripsit.* Edited by William Molesworth. 5 volumes. London: John Bohn.

Hobbes, Thomas. [1839–45] 1966. *The English Works of Thomas Hobbes of Malmesbury.* Edited by William Molesworth. 11 volumes. Germany: Scienta Verlag Aalen.

Hobbes, Thomas. [1651] 1968. *Leviathan.* Edited by C. B. Macpherson. Pelican Classics. Harmondsworth: Penguin Books.

Hobbes, Thomas. [1627] 1975. *Thucydides.* Edited by Richard Schlatter. New Brunswick: Rutgers University Press.

Horae Subsecivae: Observations and Discourses. 1620. London: Edward Blount.

Jaggard's Catalogue of English Books. Edited by Oliver H. Willard. Stanford Sudies in Language and Literature. 1914.

Johnston, David. 1986. *The Rhetoric of Leviathan: Thomas Hobbes and the Politics of Cultural Transformation.* Princeton: Princeton University Press.

Kavka, Gregory S. 1986. *Hobbesian Moral and Political Theory.* Princeton: Princeton University Press.

Kennet, White. 1708. *A Sermon Preached at the Funeral of the Right Noble William Duke of Devonshire . . . With Some Memoires of the Family Cavendish.* London: John Churchill.

Koyré, Alexander. 1957. *From the Closed World to the Infinite Universe.* Baltimore: Johns Hopkins University Press.

Laird, John. 1934. *Hobbes.* London: E. Benn.

Larsen, Wayne, Alvin C. Rencher, and Tim Layton. 1980. "Who Wrote the Book of Mormon? An Analysis of Wordprints." *BYU Studies* 20(3): 225–51.

Lipsius, Justus. 1594. *Sixe Books of Politickes or Civil Doctrine.* Translated by William Jones. London.

Machiavelli, Niccolò. 1985. *The Prince.* Translated by Harvey Mansfield, Jr. Chicago: University of Chicago Press.

Malcolm, Noel. 1981. "Hobbes, Sandys, and the Virginia Company." *The Historical Journal* 24: 297–321.

Malcolm, Noel. 1984. *De Dominis (1560–1624): Venetian, Anglican, Ecumenist and Relapsed Heretic.* London: Strickland & Scott Academic Publications.

Mansfield, Harvey, Jr. 1979. *Machiavelli's New Modes and Orders: A Study of the "Discourses of Livy."* Ithaca: Cornell University Press.

Mathews, C. Elkin. 1909. "Commentary on O'Brian." *Notes and Queries,* 10th ser., 12:164–65.

McIlwain, Charles Howard. 1918. *The Political Works of James I.* Cambridge: Harvard University Press.

McNeilly, F. S. 1968. *The Anatomy of* Leviathan. London: Macmillan.

Meinecke, Friedrich. 1957. *Machiavellism: The Doctrine of Raison d'Etat and Its Place in Modern History.* Trans. by Douglas Scott. London: Routledge & Kegan Paul.

Morton, A. Q. 1978. *Literary Detection: How to Prove Authorship and Fraud in Literature and Documents.* New York: Charles Scribner's Sons.

Moryson, Fynes. 1617. *An itinerary vvritten by Fynes Moryson gent. first in the Latine tongue, and then translated by him into English: containing his ten yeeres travell throvgh the tvvelve domjnions of Germany, Bohmerland, Sweitzerland, Netherland Denmarke, Poland, Jtaly, Turky, France, England, Scotland, and Ireland.* London: Printed by J. Beale.

Mosteller, F. W. and Wallace, D. 1964. *Inference and Disputed Authorship: The Federalist Papers.* Reading, Mass: Addison-Wesley; second edition published 1984 as Frederick Mosteller and David L. Wallace, *Applied Bayesian and Classical Inference: The Case of the Federalist Papers.* New York: Springer-Verlag.

Oakeshott, Michael. 1946. Introduction to *Leviathan,* by Thomas Hobbes. Oxford: Basil Blackwell.

O'Brien, Edward J. H. 1909. *"Horae Subsecivae 1620."Notes and Queries,* 10th ser., 12:101–3, 162–63.

Orsini, Gian Napoleone. 1936. *Bacone e Machiavelli.* Genoa: E. degli Orfini.

Orwin, Clifford. 1978. "Machiavelli's Unchristian Charity." *American Political Science Review* 72: 1217–28.

Parr, Anthony. 1992. "Thomas Coryat and the Discovery of Europe." *The Huntington Library Quarterly 55:* 578–602.

Parry, Geraint. 1971. "Review of F. O. Wolf, *Die neue Wissenschaft des Thomas Hobbes." Political Studies* 19:250–52.

Peters, Richard. 1956. *Hobbes.* Harmondsworth: Penguin Books.

Pollard, A. W., and G. R. Redgrave, comps. 1946. *Short-Title Catalogue of Books Printed in England, Scotland, & Ireland, 1475–1640.* London: The Bibliographical Society.

Praz, Mario. [1928] 1973. *Machiavelli and the Elizabethans*. Folcroft, Pa.: Folcroft Library Editions.

Raab, Felix. 1964. *The English Face of Machiavelli: A Changing Interpretation, 1500–1700*. London: Routledge & Kegan Paul.

Reynolds, Noel B. and John L. Hilton. 1992. "Statistical Wordprint Analysis Identifies New Hobbes Essays." *International Hobbes Association Newsletter*, n.s., 14:4–9.

Reynolds, Noel B. and John L. Hilton. 1994. "Thomas Hobbes and the Authorship of the *Horae Subsecivae*." *History of Political Thought* 14:361–80.

Rogow, Arnold. 1986. *Thomas Hobbes: Radical in the Service of Reaction*. New York: W. W. Norton.

Royal Commission on Historical Manuscripts. 1977. *Report on the MSS and the Papers of Thomas Hobbes (1588–1679) in the Devonshire Collections, Chatsworth, Bakewell, Derbyshire*. London: Royal Commission on Historical Manuscripts.

Sandys, George. [1615] 1632. *A relation of a journey begun An: Dom: 1610. Fovre bookes Containing a description of the Turkish empire, of Egypt, of the Holy Land, of the remote parts of Italy, and ilands adioyning*. London: Printed for R. Allot.

Saxonhouse, Arlene. 1972. "The Origins of Hobbes' Pre-Scientific Thought: An Interpretation of the *Horae Subsecivae*." Ph.D. diss., Yale University.

Saxonhouse, Arlene. 1981. "Hobbes and the *Horae Subsecivae*." *Polity* 13:541–67.

Sells, A. Lytton. 1964. *The Paradise of Travellers: The Italian Influence on Englishmen in the Seventeenth Century*. Bloomington: Indiana University Press.

Smith, M. W. A. 1985a. "An Investigation of Morton's Method to Distinguish Elizabethan Playwrights." *Computers and the Humanities* 19:3–21.

Smith, M. W. A. 1985b. "An Investigation of the Basis of Morton's Method for the Determination of Authorship." *Style* 19 (3, Fall):341–68.

Sommerville, Johann P. 1992. *Thomas Hobbes: Political Ideas in Historical Context*. New York: St. Martin's Press.

Sorrell, Tom. 1986. *Hobbes*. London: Routledge & Kegan Paul.

Stephen, Leslie. [1904] 1961. *Hobbes*. Ann Arbor: University of Michigan Press.

Stoye, John. 1952. *English Travellers Abroad: Their Influence in English Society and Politics.* London: Cape.

Strauss, Leo. [1936] 1952. *The Political Philosophy of Hobbes: Its Basis and Its Genesis.* Translated by Elsa M. Sinclair. Chicago: University of Chicago Press.

Strauss, Leo. 1958. *Thoughts on Machiavelli.* Seattle: University of Washington Press.

Talaska, Richard. 1988. "Analytic and Synthetic Method According to Hobbes." *Journal of the History of Philosophy* 26: 207–37.

Taylor, A. E. 1908. *Thomas Hobbes.* London: A. Constable.

Thomas, Keith. 1965. "The Social Origins of Hobbes's Political Thought." In *Hobbes Studies,* edited by Keith Brown. Oxford: Blackwell.

Toffanin, Giuseppe. [1921] 1972. *Machiavelli e il "Tacitismo."* Naples: Guida Editori.

Tuck, Richard. 1988. "Hobbes and Descartes." In *Perspectives on Thomas Hobbes,* edited by G. A. J. Rogers and Alan Ryan, 11–40. Oxford: Clarendon Press.

Walpole, Horace. 1806. *A Catalogue of Royal and Noble Authors of England, Scotland and Ireland; with lists of their works, enlarged and continued to the present by Thomas Park.* 5 volumes. London: Printed for John Scott.

Watkins, J. W. N. 1965. *Hobbes's System of Ideas: A Study in the Political Significance of Philosophical Theories.* London: Hutchinson.

Wolf, F. O. 1969. *Die neue Wissenschaft des Thomas Hobbes: Zu den Grundlagen der Politischen Philosophie der Neuzeit. Mit Hobbes' Essays.* Stuttgart-Bad Cannstatt: Friedrich Frommann Verlag.

Womersley, David. 1991. "Sir Henry Savile's Translation of Tacitus and Political Interpretations of Elizabethan Texts." *Review of English Studies* 42:313–42.

Wood, Anthony à. [1691–92] 1813–20. *Athenae Oxonienses.* New edition with additions by Philips Bliss. 5 volumes. London: F. C. and J. Rivington.

INDEX

Page numbers referencing Hobbes's "Discourses" are in boldface type.

Aesop's *Fables,* 37n. 11
Agrippa, Gaius, **52**
Agrippa, Lucius, **52**
Agrippa, Marcus, **41, 50–52,** 136–37
Agrippa, Postumus, **55–57, 62–63**
Alexander, tomb of, **79**
Antonius, Marcus, **36, 41–43**
Aquinas, St. Thomas, 151n
Aubrey, John, 6n. 6, 10n, 127–28, 140n
Augustus: 148; and the acquisition of power, **35–36, 41–42, 44–46,** 130, 135; and dissimulation, **53,** 136; and Livia, **55;** as a new prince, **44, 49,** 131–32, 139; as a politic prince, 135; and the problem of succession, **49–58,** 138; and the provinces, **49;** and the title of Prince, **37–38;** and the titles of power, **37–38, 43;** and the Triumvirate, **36, 43;** and war, **58–59,** 137–38
Aurelius, Marcus (statue of), **76**

Bacchus, Temple of, **78**
Bacon, Francis: 12, 13, 159, 161; as the author of essays, 124n. 2; *Essays,* 4, 5; and the *Horae Subsecivae,* 9; and Machiavelli, 129
Basilikon Doron, 131
Beal, Peter, 4n
Bellarmine, Cardinal, **96**
Blount, Edward (publisher of the *Horae Subsecivae*): 3, 8n. 10; on the authorship of the *Horae Subsecivae,* **26**
Bobbio, Norberto, 150n
Borghese, Cardinal: **95–96;** gardens of, **79, 89**
Brigham Young University, 11, 158
Bruce, Christian, 8n. 10
Bruce, Lord (Baron of Kinloss), 8n. 10
Brutus, Lucius, **32–33**
Brutus, Marcus, **41, 42**
Brydges, Grey (Lord Chandos), 8n. 10, 9
Brydges, Sir S.E., 9
Bush, Douglas, 4n
Bywaters, David, 130n. 12

Caesar, Gaius, **54**
Caesar, Julius: **35, 36, 41;** *Commentaries,* **39;** tomb of, **78**
Caesar, Lucius, **54**
Capitol (Roman), **76**
Cassius, Spurius, **44**
Cavendish, Gilbert, 9
Cavendish, William (first earl of Devonshire), 4–5, 8n. 11
Cavendish, William (second earl of Devonshire and Hobbes's tutee): 4, 8n. 11, 10; as author of a "Discourse against Flatterie," 8n. 10; as author of "Essayes," 4n. 2, 9; as author of the *Horae Subsecivae,* 7–8; and Fulgenzio Micanzio, 10n, 128n; and Hobbes, 5, 10n, 141
Cavendish family, 4, 7–8, 10n, 129n. 10
Cestius, tomb of, **78**
Chatsworth (Cavendish estate), 4–5, 10n. 14
Cicero, Marcus Tullius, **39, 115, 118**
Cinna, Lucius, **35,** 135
civil war, **37, 46–47,** 134, 149
Claudius, Appius, **34**
Claudius, Drusus, **53**
Coke, Edward, 153n
Constantine, **71–72, 86–87**
Consulship, **33, 35, 50**
control authors. *See* control texts
control texts, 11, 12, 13, 14–15, 158, 160
Coryat, Thomas, 142
Cremutius, Cordus, **41**
Crassus, Marcus, **35–36**
Cropsey, Joseph, 153n

Decemviri, **34**
Demosthenes, **107**

Dictators (Roman), **33–34**
Diocletian's Baths, **78**
discourse (as literary genre), 124n. 2, 141
"Discourse against Flatterie": 8n. 12, 9, 124n. 2; authorship of, 8n. 10, 9–10, 15
divine right, 131–32
Donation of Constantine, **72,** 72n. 2, 142
Drusus (brother of Tiberius and step-son of Augustus), **54–55**

English College (in Rome), **91–92**
essay (as literary genre), 124n. 2
"Essayes" (manuscript version of parts of the *Horae Subsecivae*): authorship of, 4, 9n; date of composition, 5
Euclid's *Elements,* 6n. 6

Fortescue, John, 107n. 7

Germanicus, Julius Gaesar, **57, 58, 66**
Greville, Fulke, 12, 13, 15, 159

Hamilton, John Jay, 4n, 8n. 12
Hardwick Hall, 8, 129n. 10
Harwood, John, 4n
Henry VIII, **80**
Heraclitus, **107,** 149–50
Hilton, John L., 9. *See also* statistical wordprinting
Hobbes, Thomas: on appearances, 135–36; on architecture, **90–91;** autobiography, 127n. 6; on the Cardinals, **96–98;** *De Cive,* 133n; continental trip, 6, 127n. 7, 141; *De Corpore,* 7n. 8; on credu-

lity, 146–47; on the decline of Augustus, **61–62;** on dissimulation, **64,** 137; *Elements of Law,* 133n; on equality, 135; on the first form of government, **31;** on flattery, **39–40;** on gardens, **91;** and the geometric method, 6–7, 125, 140–41; on giving and receiving benefits, **51;** on the growth of Rome, **32;** on immortality, **82–84;** on the just war, **59,** 137–38; on justice, **32, 108–9,** 152–53; on lethargy, **73–74;** *Leviathan,* 126, 132–33, 137, 138–39, 143, 146; on liberality, **44,** 132; on liberty, **33, 106;** on Livia, **56;** and Machiavelli, 7n. 9; *de Mirabilis Pecci,* 5; on the mixed regime, 133n; on monarchy, **33, 45–46,** 133, 133n; natural condition of mankind, 144, 149; on the new prince, **43–44,** 126, 131, 137, 139, 148; on the origin of political order, 124–26, 128, 135, 139, 150–51; on political instability, 134; on the Pope, **95–98;** on the problem of succession, **49–58,** 138; on public service, **74,** 143–45; reflections on holy antiquities, **87–88;** on Roman statuary, **76–77;** Thucydides translation, 5, 126, 139; on travel in Italy, **98–102;** on two masters, **66;** on the value of "antiquities," **80–82;** and the Virginia Company, 5n. 5; and the writing and study of history, **38–41,** 126, 139–40. *See also* civil war; *Horae Subsecivae;* law; Roman Church; Rome

Horae Subsecivae: Observations and Discourses, 3; authorship of, 7–10; Hobbesian authorship of, 4, 15–16, 19; literary style of, 124n. 2

Inquisition, **99, 101**

James I, 131–33
Johnston, David, 6n. 8
Julia (daughter of Augustus), **52**

Kennett, White, 9n
Koyré, Alexander, 124n. 1

Laocoön, statue of, **79**
law: **49;** the absence of, **106–7, 109, 110,** 149; the change of, **113–14;** and custom, **111, 118–19,** 153; the ends of, **105;** and reason, **115,** 150, 152; on the Law of Nature (natural law), **110,** 151–52; laws of nature, 151n; types of, **110, 116–17,** 151–52; variety of, **112,** 152
Lepidus, **36, 41–43**
Leviathan. See Hobbes, Thomas: *Leviathan*
Liberalism, origins of, 123–24
Lipsius, Justus, 129
Livia (wife of Augustus, mother of Tiberius), **52, 54–58,** 66
Lucretia, **33**
Lycurgus, **118**

Machiavelli, Niccolò: 139, 145; availability of in the 17th century, 131n. 14; on beneficent violence, 132; on Christianity, 144; *The Dis-*

Machiavelli, Niccolò (continued)
    courses on Livy, 124n. 2,
    129n. 9, 138, 143; on dissim-
    ulation, 136; on early Rome,
    143; and Hobbes, 7n. 9,
    124–25; on new princes,
    131; as originator of mod-
    ern political thought, 7, 125,
    133, 141; *The Prince*, 129n.
    9, 130n. 11, 136–37; as pro-
    ponent of freedom, 130n.
    11, 144; and republicanism,
    138; and Tacitus, 129, 130n.
    11
Malcolm, Noel: 4n. 2, 127n. 7;
    on Hobbes and the Virginia
    Company, 5n. 5, 116n. 32
Mann Whitney nonparametric
    statistic, 159n, 160
Mansfield, Harvey, 129n. 9
Marcellus, Claudius (nephew of
    Augustus), 49–50
Melius, Spurius, 44
Mersenne, Marin, 6n. 8
Micanzio, Fulgenzio, 10n. 128n
Michelangelo, 79, 84–85
Miracle of St. Peter's chains, 87
Mons Palatinus, 76
Mood test, 161
Morton, A. Q., 12, 159, 160
Moryson, Fynes, 141n

natural-law theory, 150–51. *See
    also* law
Nero, 76
noise, 158, 160, 161
noncontextual word patterns,
    11n, 12, 13, 14, 19, 157,
    159
nonparametric null-hypothesis
    statistical test. *See* null-
    hypothesis rejections
null-hypothesis rejections, 13n,
    14, 15n, 159–60

Oakeshott, Michael, 5

Pantheon, 77–78
Parr, Anthony, 142n. 20
Parry, Geraint, 4n
Parsons, Robert, 91, 101, 101n.
    55
Paul III, 76
Paul V, 85, 95–97
Peloponnesian War, 127
Plato, 106, 149, 150
*Politicorum, sive, Civilis doctrinal
    libris sex,* 129
Pompey, Gnaeus, 35–36, 41
Pope's Palace, 85
Popes, 72
Principate, 130–33, 139
Protestant Reformation, 129
Provinces, Roman, 47, 48, 49

Regifugium, 33
Republic (Roman): 60; and lib-
    erty, 132, 134–35; as model
    of instability, 134, 149
Republicanism, 138
Reynolds, Noel B., 9
Rogow, Arnold A., 4n
Roman Church: Hobbes's cri-
    tique of, 97–98, 147; as polit-
    ical institution, 94–95, 147
Roman law, 116–18, 153
Rome (the city): 71–72,
    141–42; beginnings of, 32;
    government in the 17th cen-
    tury, 94; topography of, 73,
    143
Romulus, 32, 118

Saint John's Church, 86–87
Saint Paul's Church, 86
Saint Peter's Church, 84
Santa Croce, 86
Santa Maria Maggiore, 85
Saxonhouse, Arlene W., 19

Seneca, statue of, **80**
signal, 161
Stationer's Register, 8
statistical wordprinting: 10–19, 157–62; analysis procedures, general, 12, for the Hobbes study, 12–15; compared to fingerprinting, 11, 157; English authors control group (*see* control texts), John Hilton model, 11, 16, 19, 158–60; lack of scholarly consensus on, 10–11, 157–58, 161–62; psycholinguistic explanation of, 11, 157; results of *Horae Subsecivae* study, 15–19, 158, 160–61; success of, 11, 157, 161–62; use of computers in, 11, 158
Strauss, Leo: on the authorship of the *Horae Subsecivae,* 4n, 5; discovery of "Essayes," 7; on Hobbes's preferred form of government, 133n; on the *Horae Subsecivae,* 4; on Machiavelli, 124–25, 129n. 9; on the moral foundation of Hobbes's thought, 5, 6n. 7, 6n. 8, 145n; on the origins of modern political thought, 124–25
stylometry, 161. *See also* statistical wordprinting
subsecivae (meaning of), 3n
Sulla, Lucius, **35,** 135

Tacitism, 130
Tacitus: **31, 62, 107,** 126, 139; *Annales,* 126–30, 133, 138;

Histories, **51,** 128, 129n. 9; Hobbes on, **62;** as Machiavellian, 129–30; popularity in 17th century, 128; as republican, 129–30; translations of, 128; on writing history, **40,** 140
Tarquinius Superbus, **32**
Thomas, Keith, 145n
Thompson, Francis (former librarian at Chatsworth), 5n. 4, 8n. 11, 9n
Thucydides, 126–27
Tiberius, **53–58, 62–66,** 137–38
Toffanin, Giuseppe, 129–30
Tosco, Cardinal, **96–97**
Trajan, **78**
Travel literature (16th and 17th century), 141–42
Tribunes, **35, 43**
Triumvir, as title, **43,** 136
Triumvirate (Antonius, Lepidus, and Augustus), **36, 42, 46**

Ulpian, **119**

Vatican, **85**
Vespasian, **77**
Virgil, *Aeneid,* 79

Walpole, Horace, 9
Wheldon, James (Hobbes's amanuensis), 8
Wolf, F. O., 4n
Womersley, David, 130n. 11
wordprint. *See* statistical wordprinting

Zwicker, Steven N., 130n. 12